# the WRITE to READ

*To my family—my husband, Chuck, and my children, Meg and Matt, who spoke "book"*
*with me for over a year and who continue to inspire me,*
*by example, to follow my passion.*

# the WRITE to READ

*Response*
*Journals*
*That*
*Increase*
*Comprehension*

LESLEY ROESSING

*Foreword by*

*Alan Lawrence Sitomer*

CORWIN
A SAGE Company

*For information:*

Corwin
A SAGE Company
2455 Teller Road
Thousand Oaks, California 91320
(800) 233-9936
Fax: (800) 417-2466
www.corwinpress.com

SAGE Ltd.
1 Oliver's Yard
55 City Road
London EC1Y 1SP
United Kingdom

SAGE India Pvt. Ltd.
B 1/I 1 Mohan Cooperative Industrial Area
Mathura Road, New Delhi 110 044
India

SAGE Asia-Pacific Pte. Ltd.
33 Pekin Street #02-01
Far East Square
Singapore 048763

Printed in the United States of America.

*Library of Congress Cataloging-in-Publication Data*

Roessing, Lesley.
The write to read: response journals that increase comprehension / Lesley Roessing.
    p. cm.
Includes bibliographical references and index.
ISBN 978-1-4129-7426-4 (pbk.)
    1. Language arts (Secondary)—United States. 2. Reading comprehension—United States. 3. Reading promotion—United States. 4. Diaries—Authorship. I. Title.

LB1631.R575 2009
428.4071'2—dc22                                      2009014367

This book is printed on acid-free paper.

11   12   13   10   9   8   7   6   5   4   3   2

| | |
|---|---|
| *Acquisitions Editor:* | Hudson Perigo |
| *Editorial Assistant:* | Lesley K. Blake |
| *Production Editor:* | Cassandra Margaret Seibel |
| *Copy Editor:* | Paula L. Fleming |
| *Typesetter:* | C&M Digitals (P) Ltd. |
| *Proofreader:* | Marleis Roberts |
| *Cover Designer:* | Anthony Paular |
| *Graphic Designer:* | Scott Van Atta |

# Contents

# List of Figures

# List of Photographs

# Foreword

Lesley Roessing has written a book filled with excellent ideas as to how to improve reading comprehension through response journaling; she presents them in a way that is smart, accessible, and practical. Filled with tools, tips, and strategies—plus loads of student examples—I am *sold!* This book has improved not only my insight into the reading/writing connection but my ability to translate this new knowledge directly into my classroom practice.

Alan Lawrence Sitomer
California Teacher of the Year 2007 and Bestselling Author of
*The Hoopster*
*Homeboyz*
*The Secret Story of Sonia Rodriguez*
*Teaching Teens & Reaping Results*
*Hip-Hop High School*
*Hip-Hop Poetry and The Classics*

# Preface

I wrote this book for teachers like me who are committed to help students increase reading comprehension. Over the years, I observed in classrooms, workshops, conference presentations, and graduate education classes that I was a fairly typical teacher. My students would read a literary work and answer questions as they went along—questions from resources either provided by the publisher, found in workbooks at teachers' stores, generated by a district committee, or created by me. However, I was never really satisfied with this approach. Most resources encouraged reader responses that did not allow for individuality or creativity, and it was difficult to tell if students were reading or just copying each other's answers. My students were not being asked to interact with text on personal levels.

A few years ago, I was introduced to the concept of reading workshop, in which students read self-selected texts. They would read in class but also read independently as homework. I wondered how I could generate assessments for each book and know that students were really reading. With readers reading divergent texts, what could I assess? How could I ascertain my students' strengths and weaknesses? Their instructional needs? How could I tell if they comprehended, and how I could help them increase that comprehension? I looked for alternatives to existing assessment practices.

I read Louise Rosenblatt's theory of reader response. I realized how readers construct meaning through their transactions with text, and I recognized the value of response. And so, I directed students "to respond." Dutifully, they either retold the text or looked at me blankly, pens in hand. I realized that, just like any skill or knowledge, response has to be taught and must be guided. Not only do students need to be invited to respond personally, but response instruction needs to be incorporated into the teaching of reading strategies and expanded and refined throughout the year.

With that goal in mind, I planned a yearlong response curriculum, training students to respond to their reading in a variety of ways, moving toward more proficient and more meaningful reflection and moving from teacher-directed control of response to student-directed choice. I designed a program to give my students the tools they needed to assume control of their responses. I then connected the types of responses to the divergent genres and modes of reading and integrated response formats into my language arts curriculum, which includes whole-class shared texts, small-group shared texts (book clubs), and individual reading. I also paired response formats to the reading strategies that I was teaching. I created a Response Journal for students to use, to which I add as the year progresses. These Reading Journals allow my readers and me to keep track of their reading and respond throughout the year.

I found that students not only appreciated that their personal responses had validity, but they welcomed the variety of responses. Adolescents need variety for two reasons: to hold their interest and, after they have mastered the skills, to give them choices. At the end of the year, my students reflected that they saw the relevance of the different responses and the responses' connection to their texts, and most admitted that the practice had made them more perceptive, insightful readers. Creative ways to respond also appeared to engage reluctant readers.

Each year since, I have included new ways to respond to a variety of texts, honing the process so that the form of response correlates to the focus of each of my reading lessons. By the end of the year, students have been exposed to numerous response formats, and I have been most impressed with how readers have been able to choose the most appropriate ways to respond as they read their individual texts. In cases where I created forms for particular types of response, students have asked me to make all available so that they could choose which ones they wanted to use at different times and with different readings. By the end of each year, students were responding as experienced readers.

A Response Journal is a means through which I can observe the reading thoughts of each student. I am able to confer weekly through the Journals, and truly no child is left behind. The students appreciate the one-to-one communication, and I can tell that they are aware that I am reading by some of the personal comments made to me.

In addition, response journaling gives me a basis for assessment—both formative and evaluative. The record of reading preserved in their Reading Journals provides my students a basis for metacognition about their reading. In this way, adolescents are able to begin taking responsibility for their own learning.

Many times during presentations and teacher workshops, teachers have confided that they are aware of the need for reader response but are not clear about how to begin and how to develop response throughout the school year. Even teachers who already teach or require reading response disclose that they do not have a yearlong plan; they create one response form and use it throughout the year—for all texts and for all students. This approach does not scaffold the teaching of response. It does not take into account individual readers or different types of literature. It also does not promote better comprehension of text.

I wrote *The Write to Read* to meet the needs of teachers who want to employ some type of program of reader response. The book can be used as a practical handbook to enhance students' reading comprehension. It presents a unique, yearlong plan for encouraging and teaching reader response in the middle and high school classroom. Most activities and lessons are appropriate or adaptable for younger students and for both language arts and content area classes. The book contains a blend of theory, practice, practical advice, models, and student samples from my classes.

I teach both heterogeneous and accelerated eighth-grade language arts classes in a suburban community. The skills and activities in this book are demonstrated in language arts classes that each have a yearlong reading workshop plan focusing on gradual release of control through a continuum of shared readings (short stories, poetry, nonfiction articles, a play, and a novel) to small-group readings (book clubs) to individual readings; however, all skills and activities presented are adaptable to language arts or English classes following any reading curriculum.

I have described in this book what I do in my classroom. Each response mode is introduced with a teacher-designed model and reinforced with student-created samples. Significant space has been devoted to examples because of the importance of modeling to scaffolding. In my experience, I have found that modeling does not inhibit the creativity of those who have the skills and that students who "copy" models are those who may lack the confidence to attempt the task at all. This book addresses how to assist struggling readers and writers and build their confidence; as they feel more secure, they should produce work of higher quality and greater quantity. Teachers, especially those of different grade levels or content areas, will find in this book effective ways to create their own models or utilize examples from their own students. Models and ideas for adaptations to content area classes are included in Chapter 10.

*The Write to Read* illustrates how, after a lesson and model is introduced and explained, the students are led in a guided practice, either collaboratively or individually, and the results are shared with a partner, a small group, or the entire class. Students are then expected to try the response, when fitting, with at least one reading that week. After mastery, readers are encouraged to employ the different response methods *where* and *when* appropriate throughout the year. Forms for this purpose are discussed in the corresponding chapters. Reproducible materials for teacher use are included in Resource B so that teachers may adapt them for their own purposes.

This book presents literacy tools to train readers to respond to their reading with the primary intent of improving comprehension in a yearlong, scaffolded curriculum. Methods and activities, however, can be used individually. These ideas can be integrated into a reading workshop approach, a designated shared-text curriculum, and language arts or content area classes. While written primarily for Grades 5 through 12, ideas in this book are adaptable to elementary classroom and for differentiated instruction. The primary goal of the book is to help teachers plan for, implement, and evaluate students' divergent text understanding and enjoyment, and it is aimed at promoting and enhancing response to text and engagement in reading, especially of those students who may need some guidance in engaging in reflective text reading and response.

# Acknowledgments

With appreciation and recognition to . . .

- My students, past and present, who were willing to attempt every assignment I gave them even if they, or I, were not certain of the outcome. They persevered with me as I researched, experimented, and assessed. I am indebted to them for making me the best teacher I can be so that I might help them become the best readers they can be. Their Reading Journals provided the student examples for this book, and their comments, candid as only adolescents can be, provided the commentary. I appreciate their willingness in letting me share their written and oral responses with the readers of this book.

- My student Andrew Karahalis who put a name to our experiences in the reading classroom (and this book).

- Doug Tyson, colleague (and a former student of mine), who captured the joy of reading through his photographs of my students.

- My family members, who all write, read, and celebrate literacy daily and, most of all, support my writing and reading. They have patiently listened to lesson plans and stories of adolescent reading and writing for over 20 years.

- My parents, who engendered a love of reading in me; throughout my youth, I rarely saw them without a book or magazine in hand.

- Carol Raymond, a friend who not only gave me her support but loaned her fifth-grade science class to demonstrate that these techniques are not just for adolescents.

- Helen and Braden Montgomery, friends and colleagues who read the draft manuscript and provided insight into the use of this book for high school and college classes.

- Diane Dougherty, my mentor and friend, who helped me find my inner writer and facilitated my transformation from a literature teacher to a reading teacher.

- Linda Pollum, Ridley Middle School librarian, who taught me the power of a good book talk.

- Art Peterson, of the National Writing Project and one of my first editors, who taught me how to revise effectively. Art has continued to support my writing.

- NCTE's Kurt Austin, who told me to "write it" when I told him that teachers wanted to know more about reader response and, in so doing, was the catalyst for this project. Also NMSA's Ed Brazee, who encouraged me to turn my ideas into a finished manuscript.

- The Ridley School District Administration Team:

  o Chas Maiers, Ridley Middle School's wonderfully supportive principal, who continually encourages my efforts to balance teaching, writing, and presenting and who values reading, his staff, and our students. He is a constant encouraging presence in our classrooms, observing students as they display new skills, innovative techniques, and/or creative endeavors;

  o Assistant principal Denea Klisch, who always takes an interest in my never-ending "projects," both in and out of the classroom; and

  o Superintendent Dr. Nick Ignatuk, a frequent guest at my students' presentations.

- The Corwin Team, a joy with whom to work:

  o Hudson Perigo and Lesley Blake, who not only made this book possible but made the experience pleasurable (and who "held my hand" long-distance throughout the process);

  o Cassandra Seibel, who shepherded my manuscript attentively through every step of production;

  o Paula Fleming, who copyedited with professionalism and care but also with sensitivity to both my feelings and my vision; and

  o those whose names I don't know who helped form a bridge from my ideas to teachers seeking to increase their students' comprehension of, and pleasure in, reading.

# About the Author

 **Lesley Roessing** has spent 20 years teaching eighth-grade language arts and humanities in suburban Philadelphia. Prior to discovering her interest in teaching middle school students, she taught high school English. Over the past six years, she has published articles in *English Journal* and *Voices from the Middle* (National Council of Teachers of English), *The Quarterly* (National Writing Project), and *Middle School Journal* and *Middle Ground* (National Middle School Association). In addition, Lesley has presented her articles and ideas widely in a variety of formats, from lecturing at annual conferences of teachers' associations to teaching workshops for local organizations and schools. In 2002, Lesley became a writing and, in 2004, a literature teacher-consultant for the Pennsylvania Writing & Literature Project, where she began her metamorphosis from a literature teacher into a reading teacher who opens adolescents' eyes to the wonder of literature and from a composition teacher to a writer who shares the gift of writing with her students, both for its own value and to enhance their reading experiences.

# The Three Rs

## *Rationale for Reader Response*

*December 2008*

Dear Mom,

This year we have learned a whole new way of responding by journal entries. It really helps you think about what you're reading, and since it is all on paper you can always go back and think about things you have changed about your reading in the past. What we usually write about is like a little bit of a summary, not too much though, then we talk about some of the strategies we used and what we were thinking while reading. I like it a lot because I get to see what I thought before I read the book and then after.

Hollie

I have always encouraged my students to read. The consensus of the research as well as my experience is that the more students read, the better they read. However, I have found that to a great extent, that conclusion depends on the definition of *better*. I agree that students will read more fluently, but first we have to examine what *reading* is. Many students think they are reading because they can understand the words and then summarize the plot or, in the case of nonfiction, find the facts. But teachers need to recognize if their students really comprehend what they are reading. If not, teachers must distinguish where the breakdown occurs and identify how they can help students take comprehension to a more profound level. Many students do not automatically advance to more challenging material or push themselves to think about their reading on different levels. Adolescents can read without awareness—unconscious of literary devices, inattentive to writer's craft, lacking insight of comprehension skills they are using. In other words, they read without *interacting* with the text.

A reader response program allows teachers to see how readers make meaning from what they read and whether they are truly engaged in what they are reading, and it allows teachers to help students read authentically.

Authentic reading is interactive. A few years ago, I became familiar with Louise Rosenblatt's reader response theory. As Jeffrey Wilhelm (1997) explains it, "reading is a 'transaction' in which the reader and the text converse together in a particular situation to make meaning" (p. 19). In other words, readers construct meaning from their transactions with the text. Teaching that focuses on finding the "correct" answers or interpretations or deciphering teacher meaning is efferent, or informational, reading. In teaching students to experience, to enjoy, and to claim ownership of literature—or, as Rosenblatt would say, to read *aesthetically*—one must not try to control the reader's response.

For years I *taught* novels. I told the students what to see, how to interpret, what the text meant. I gave tests, and students dutifully spat back my insights. I was testing their listening, not their learning. I remember congratulating one student, Richard, for earning the highest grade on a test about a novel. I was mortified when he admitted to the class that he had never opened the book; he'd just listened and given me back what I said in class "discussions."

As a result of this type of teaching, students feel that they have to search not for *a* but for *the* meaning of a text. They surmise that there is One True Meaning and only teachers hold that meaning. Instead, we must all acknowledge that there are many meanings. "Literary meaning is largely an individual engagement . . . it results from the creative effort of a reader working from a text" (Probst, 1994, p. 41). Rosenblatt (2005b) wrote, "There are no generic readers or generic interpretations, but only innumerable relationships between readers and texts." She continued, "Traditional and formulist methods of teaching literature treat it as a body of information to be transmitted, rather than as experiences to be reflected upon. . . . Teachers often forget that if students know they will be tested primarily on factual aspects of the work (often by multiple-choice questions) a full aesthetic reading is prevented, and the 'mix' [of public and private or personal relationship with the text] swings toward the efferent [nonliterary, factual] end of the continuum" (pp. 17–18).

Gone are my lists of questions, the lists of points that *must* be covered. I let readers engage with the text on their own playing fields. How can literature be life altering and lead to self-discovery, as it has for me, if I am inserting my life and values between the literature and the reader. Where does the reader fit in?

> No one else can read a literary work for us. The benefits of literature can emerge only from creative activity on the part of the reader himself. He responds to the little black marks on the page or to the sounds of the words in his ear and he makes something of them. The verbal symbols enable him to draw on his past experiences with what the words point to in life and literature. The text presents these words in a new and unique pattern. Out of these he is enabled actually to mold a new experience, the literary work. (Rosenblatt, 1938/2005a, p. 27)

Response theory provides that understanding best begins when students clarify and reflect on text with their own *unique* and immediate impressions. However, students need to be guided to make valid responses. Rosenblatt (1978) defines "valid" response as "an interpretation [that] is not contradicted by any element of the text, and . . . nothing is projected for which there is no verbal basis" (p. 115). Even though readers are free to make unique and personal responses, they need to base their interpretations on their understanding of the actual text. Robert Probst (1994) suggests that teachers design instruction to incorporate certain principles, such as "invite response to the text," "give students time to shape and take confidence in their responses," and "let the talk build and grow as naturally as possible, encouraging an organic flow for the discussion" (p. 42).

Teachers have to teach readers to respond—not what to respond but how to respond. Not all readers do this automatically, just as some do not automatically use reading strategies. I have asked students, "What do you think?" and received blank stares as if to say, "I think what we just read." I am reminded of Charlie Gordon in "Flowers for Algernon": when asked what he thinks when looking at an inkblot, he says, "I think an inkblot!" The difference is that our students have the intelligence to imagine and interpret. We need to scaffold response technique as well as response procedure just as we scaffold anything else we teach. I teach students how to respond, modeling different types of response. I build upon, and vary, the types and amount of response based on what they respond so that, at the end of the school year, students choose ways of responding they feel are appropriate to the text and the situation.

With this in mind, I have devised a yearlong curriculum of response journaling. The curriculum is based on two premises: (1) teachers need to teach readers how to journal, and (2) teachers need to give readers choice. Throughout the year, I teach students a variety of journaling techniques so that readers learn to respond in diverse ways, realizing their response options. These lessons give them the tools they need to assume control of their own learning. I want them to know that it is appropriate to respond in divergent ways to different types of text and to different readings and at different times in their reading lives. It is important that they experience all the options so they know the alternatives from which they can choose. By the end of the year, most students identify their favorite type of response or become skilled at modifying their

**Photo 1.1**    Matt writes a response in his reading journal

journaling to fit a particular reading. The purpose of response journaling is reader reflection; the goal is better comprehension and a more profound understanding of text.

There are five key reasons for requiring written response:

1. *To make response second-nature.* I tell students that writing responses is somewhat artificial. After I read, I do not usually write down my responses. Instead, I think them; I may discuss them with others. I tell my students that this is a training time. I also explain that when they write their responses, I am able to read them, which leads to the second reason for requiring response . . .

2. *To make individual assessment, both formative and evaluative, possible,* and then . . .

3. *To allow for metacognition.* Response journals allow students to reflect upon and respond to their thinking, thus permitting self-assessment. As William Zinsser (1988) says in *Writing to Learn,* "We write to find out what we know and what we want to say" (p. viii). He adds the point that "writing and thinking and learning cannot be separated. One cannot happen without the others" (p. 11). I explain to my students that we write to find out what we are thinking, to work out the kinks, to take us deeper as we unravel our thoughts . . .

4. *To increase comprehension.* As the 2000 report of the National Reading Panel states, "Teaching students to use . . . writing to organize their ideas about what they are reading is a proven procedure that enhances comprehension for text" (p. 4–103). And finally . . .

5. *When students write, they are reading.* Conversely, when students are reading, they are not typically writing. An added bonus of reading response is that students frequently write in conjunction with their reading. This form of writing is new for many, and it can lead the way to other, more formal writings, including critical writing.

In this era of high-stakes testing, an additional bonus is that students will become comfortable writing different types of responses to text, a major component of standardized reading tests.

While the importance of response cannot be minimized, Regie Routman (2000) counsels,

Literature extensions, when we do employ them, must be worthwhile (not merely busywork) and expand students' meaningful involvement with the text.
Meaningful literature extensions—

- develop naturally from the literature,
- thoughtfully encourage students to reexamine and reconsider the text,
- demonstrate what the reader has gleaned from the text,
- deepen students' understanding of the literary piece,
- promote connections between the text and the students' lives, BUT
- are secondary to reading for meaning and pleasure. (p. 72)

With that admonition ("secondary to reading for meaning and pleasure") in mind, I keep my response time requirements simple. My students are required to read at least 25 minutes per night, 5 nights per week, and for each reading session they are to respond for 5 minutes. Therefore, response is no more than 15 percent of their actual reading time. The goal is to not stop readers from reading because they "have" to write, so I encourage them to make the writing meaningful and even fun and keep it to a minimum. In most cases, these are draft writings. I tell students that their writing must be legible but need not be edited and certainly not revised. They are to concentrate on their reflections, not the writing product. They can write after they read so they do not interrupt aesthetic enjoyment, unless they would rather "stop and jot."

Readers are capturing raw thoughts before, during, and after reading whole texts. These writings help them to become reflective readers, which, in turn, increases their comprehension, as well as assisting me—and them—to evaluate their reading and comprehension. In a quote many have attributed to philosopher Edmund Burke, "Reading without reflecting is like eating without digesting."

# PART I

## Before-Reading Response

# 2

# The Pre-Reading Response

looked at Jen's Reading Record:

*A Child Called "It"*—abandoned

*Monster*—abandoned

Two books abandoned in a row, the first after one chapter, the other after one night's reading. It was not difficult to diagnose the problem. Obviously, Jen picked up the books—whether because of other students' hasty recommendations or because the titles caught her eye—without enough information and reflection on whether they were the right books for her. I have also heard students talking about plowing through books they "didn't like." With self-selection and individual choice, why would students read books they didn't like?

I realized that not only would I have to teach my students how to choose a book but oblige the students to look at their choices more thoroughly and reflect on how and why they were choosing books *before* they read them.

## HOW TO CHOOSE A BOOK

First, we brainstormed the ways we choose books. The students came up with the following list:

Recommendations of friends, relatives, teachers, librarian

Authors (of other books read)

Genre

Topic

Book reviews

Sequels or prequels to books read

The central problem or conflict

Setting

Types of characters

Tone

Gifts

Movies based on books or books based on movies

Reading level

Number of pages

Size of print

Titles and/or covers

I added a few that they had not thought of or that had not, so far, pertained to their reading:

Authors whom I have met or heard speak

Awards won

I then talked about books I had chosen and read based on some of these categories:

Recommendation: *The Five People You Meet in Heaven*

Author (of other books read): Jodi Picoult, *My Sister's Keeper—Nineteen Minutes*

Genre: Free verse poetry story—*Jump Ball*

Topic: Holocaust—*Milkweed*

Review: *The Things They Carried*

Sequel or prequel: *Pigs in Heaven*, sequel to *The Bean Trees*

Problem: Anorexia—*Perfect*

Setting: Tuscany, Italy—*Under the Tuscan Sun*

Character: Miss Marple—Agatha Christie mysteries

Tone: Humor—Bill Bryson's books, such as *The Life and Times of the Thunderbolt Kid*

Gift: *Tuesdays with Morrie*

Movie based on book or book based on movie: *The DaVinci Code*

Reading level: *Stuck in Neutral* (I read books written on different reading levels so that I can recommend them to diverse student readers.)

Title and/or cover: *So B. It*

Author I've met or heard speak: Sonya Sonnes—*Stop Pretending*

Awards: Pulitzer Prize winner *Maus*

The students filled in their charts and discussed with their partners books they had read and when different methods of choosing books had or had not been effective. They realized that some criteria almost always led to good reads (author, sequels, recommendations of good friends), some usually were effective (topics they were interested in, genre), and some were less predictable (book reviews, awards, title, and covers). They acknowledged that gift books or recommendations were more effective when provided by others who really knew them as readers; there were many horror stories of books bought by family members and recommendations by teachers or librarians who hadn't taken the time to get to know them as readers. Jen then admitted that she had only looked at the title of *Monster* and assumed it was a horror book, a genre she loves. This is one reason I shelve my library by genre; in my library, *Monster* by Walter Dean Myers is shelved under the heading "Street Life."

## THE ANTICIPATION RESPONSE

The next day, I took the selection process a step farther. I gave each student a book from my classroom library. They were to look at the front covers, the titles, and the authors, writing anticipation responses about what these invoked. They were then to read the back covers or inside flaps, make some additional responses and/or revise their comments. Finally, they were to read the first page or so, continuing to write their reactions. I wrote the following steps on the board:

1a. Look at the front cover: title and any subtitles, author's name, artwork, or pictures.

1b. Write a response—anything you are thinking, feeling, predicting, or questioning.

2a. Look at the back cover and any inside flap. Read the excerpt or summary, reviews, author biographical sketch.

2b. Continue your response, adding to or revising any previous thoughts.

3a. Read 1–2 pages, noting author's style, tone, word choice, and reading level.

3b. Add to your response, modifying any speculations.

We next discussed the types of comments they had written down. As a model, I went first, using a blend of adult fiction and young adult novels that I have read.

Showing a front cover, I revealed that, when a student recommended *The Five People You Meet in Heaven,* I assumed that it would be a religious book and anticipated that it would not interest me. However, because Beth asked me to read it, I did, and it became one of my favorite books because of the plot and the writing style. If I had to categorize the genre, I would say it is a blend of fantasy and inspirational. I also showed the class titles and cover art that enticed me to read a book, such as *Define Normal.* Class volunteers noted that, when they looked at the covers and titles of their novels, they found themselves making predictions about the books, especially the topics; some happened to be correct, but some were not. Jen had come this far when she chose *Monster*.

When students looked at the authors' names, they noted if they had read books, or even short stories, by those authors. In some cases, this was a positive indicator; sometimes it was a negative. This technique introduced the advantage of reading short story anthologies, such as those edited by Don Gallo, to discover if students would like certain authors. On the other hand, I recounted instances where I liked one book by an author but disliked other books by the same author, and I pointed out that sometimes a reader's interest in the topic overrides an author's writing style and vice versa.

The back cover or flaps of hardback books usually present some information about the author and provide either a short synopsis or an excerpt. I cautioned that the synopses are not written by the author and, therefore, are not indicative of the author's writing style and sometimes are not entirely accurate. I remembered the group of students who chose *Habibi* for their book club, thinking it would be more of a love story than it was; they enjoyed the book but were disappointed that it didn't live up to the romantic "promises" of the cover blurb. We took a class vote on how many would read their books based on the summary or the excerpt and discussed which of the two was more effective and why. Students observed that the excerpts intrigued them but did not give them an idea of the story. One student pointed out that sometimes movie trailers contain *all* the good, or funny, scenes and the same might be true with book blurbs. Many thought that the synopses gave them a better idea of the plot. Some noted that their covers also included reviews but discounted their influence, pointing out, "Of course they would not print any negative reviews on the cover."

Students found that reading a page or two of the book was very important, especially those books whose covers did not contain an excerpt, because from those pages they determined the book's readability and author's writing style. After even a few pages, readers could anticipate tone, diction, point of view, and verb tense. I shared my response to the book I was examining. "This book is written in present tense. I prefer books written in past tense to those in present tense where I feel like I have to keep up with the action, although I have noticed that, so far in this book, the present tense is not as intrusive as it is in some novels. That must be due to the author's writing style. Therefore, I don't think it would bother me. In some novels, I haven't noticed the verb tense until well into the book. I point out these discrepancies to illustrate that 'you can't always judge a book by its cover.'"

If there is additional time, I have students pass their books to other students, examine the new books, and respond again. I do this for several reasons. First, those students who felt they did the activity "wrong" just experienced modeling of ways they can respond— from me and from other class members. Second, I plan it so every other book has an excerpt or a summary on the cover and that there is an assortment of hardbacks and paperbacks; this way, readers become aware of the different places to look for information. I usually stick to fiction, saving nonfiction books for another pass. Another rationale for a second book is that now each student has someone close by who has also examined the book with whom to discuss it.

Last, this activity serves as an introduction to the "book pass," an activity that we hold every few weeks during the school year to familiarize students with the classroom library and with books they may wish to read. In book passes, I give each student a random book from our library. Students look at the front covers, read the back covers or

**Photo 2.1**   Brianne responds to her reading in her journal

the inside flaps, flip through the books, and read the first page. I allow about two minutes per book. If they think that they might want to read any particular books in the future, they add the books to their book pass chart. If students want to check out a book, they substitute other library books for those they want to check out. They then pass their books to the next student. We pass about ten books every week or so. Sometimes, rather than doing a whole-class pass, students sit in groups by genre—either a genre that interests them or one they have not yet tried—and conduct mini passes of books from that genre.

I compare choosing books to choosing a date or a friend. The readers typically will be spending two to four weeks with their books. It is important that they know their options (the library) and their choices (individual books).

The next day, I show the students my before-reading, or anticipation, response to *The Glass Castle* and the format I want them to use with each new book they choose to read (see Figure 2.1).

Students observe that I reflected on how I chose the book and noted my thoughts in response to the covers and the first page. They also noticed that I already had many questions and some predictions. Someone pointed out that even *at this point* I seem very interested in the book. I mention that the questions and predictions indicate that I am involved enough to have a good chance of not abandoning the book (although I will be more certain after I read a chapter or two). I also point out that, even though my response looks like a lot of writing, it took me only five minutes because I wrote what I was thinking as I examined the book and read a page. Sometimes when students look at that much writing, they assume it took much longer to write because they are thinking of how long it would take them to write that much in a constructive writing assignment.

Students then try a pre-reading or, as I call it, anticipation response of their own. They base their anticipation response on one of the books they previewed the day before, or if

| Figure 2.1 | Sample: Before-Reading Response |

**The Glass Castle by Jeanette Walls**
**Anticipation Response**

Choosing the book:

- This book was **recommended** by my friend Rose. She reads a lot, and I have liked the books she has lent me. Rose told me a little about the plot; she made the book sound interesting.

- I looked at the **cover** and saw that
    1. it was a *New York Times* bestseller, which means that many other people at least bought it, and it won two awards.
    2. it is a memoir. I like books based on the author's life, and I especially like memoirs.

The covers:

- The **title** *The Glass Castle* makes me think of fairytales and, in particular, "Cinderella." But it also makes me think of something that easily breaks. Is it symbolic**?**

- The **picture** on the front must be the author as a young girl, and the picture on the back is her now.

- The **summary** says the family was "dysfunctional but vibrant" and supports this statement with examples of the father's behaviors. Sounds like an oxymoron, which intrigues me. I wonder about the mother. It says that the children had to take care of themselves. Why**?** How**?**

- Reminds me of the novel *Monkey Island.* The picture of the author **on the back** makes her look pretty "put together"; she doesn't look like she was a neglected child.

Page 1:

- Wow! Her mother is homeless—now! The author obviously has money because Park Avenue (New York City) is very expensive, and her apartment has a doorman. How did she go from being a child who took care of herself to a New York socialite**?** Why isn't she going to the party? Why do her parents *want* to be homeless**?** Her mother doesn't sound crazy—she sounds idealistic.

- I **predict** that this is told with a flashback since it starts in the present time.

time allows, I pass out new books. They share portions of their responses, and I collect them to evaluate how they did. I can make suggestions and comments and return them before they choose their first books.

This type of pre-reading response becomes a requirement. Before-reading response leads readers to choose books based on personal criteria and to reflect on their choices; reflection compels them to think about the book before they invest significant time, which they will lose if they abandon their books. Hopefully, it also reduces the number of "abandoned books." I have found that some students have trouble with the term *anticipation response,* so I also refer to a *preview response,* a term sometimes more comprehensible to them.

The assignment looks like Figure 2.2.

| Figure 2.2 | Anticipation Response Assignment |

**The Anticipation Response**

Choose a book and respond to the following:

- Title
- Author
- Cover art
- Genre
- Any synopsis or excerpt on the back cover or inside jacket
- Anything else that grabs your interest (flip through book)—for example, number of pages, length, chapters, pictures, reading level, font, print size, subheadings
- First few pages of text (your 25-minute reading for that day)

Kaitlyn wrote her first anticipation response on the book *Stop Pretending* by Sonya Sones:

### How I Chose this Book

I chose this because Mrs. Roessing recommended it to the class. It sounded good when she described some of it. So I checked out the book that day.

*Stop Pretending* is a true story; I enjoy reading this kind of genre. Also it is written in the form of poetry, and I love reading, and I like to compose, poetry as well. The writing was somewhat large, and the pages were small. There were not too many pages. It has two of the kinds of genre I like to read in it so I chose it mostly because of that. Also, basing it on who recommended it, since my teacher recommended it, it must be a pretty good book.

### Anticipation Response

The title *Stop Pretending* made me think that someone is not being the true self that they are or someone knows something but that person just won't tell. The author Sonya Sones I have never heard of before, but I need to expand my varieties of authors so I chose to read something by someone new. The cover of a girl taking a picture, then another picture of the girl doing the same thing, but all messed up made me realize something must be messed up with her life or something has gone seriously wrong. The back shows that it is in a poetic form about a crazy girl; the writing looked well written also.

Page 1. Interesting. It is about this girl who is my age whose older sister goes crazy Christmas Eve. What a surprise this must have been for her parents! This changes everything; it seems the sister doesn't notice what happened to her. This is weird; she doesn't even realize it . . . how? It seems good so far, so let's see!

From this response, I can see that Kaitlyn established criteria on which to base her choice of reading material and that she took her time before making her decision. She also provided herself with a purpose to read, a valuable reading strategy.

During the year, the anticipation responses become shorter, as it became second nature for students to examine a book and think about the criteria on which they were basing that selection. For example, in midyear, Taylor chose a book about the Holocaust and wrote her anticipation response:

> I chose to read *Your Name is Renee* because mostly the cover. When I saw the young girl's sad eyes, I wanted to know what pain and hardships were behind them. When I read the first few pages, I found I liked the author's description when saying things like "The small innocent face smiling up at me, I could never bring myself to tell such tragedy." This type of writing made me think of how hard it must be too young. Overall, the writing caught my attention immediately. I think in the novel as it progresses, Renee/Ruth will help many get through hardships of the Holocaust. I am anxious to read more about the process the characters go through.

While students still occasionally abandon books, they do so less frequently.

## ADAPTATIONS

For struggling readers, I make a form containing the topics in the assignment above, reminding them to look over their choices and to what stimuli they should respond. Just the act of requiring readers to "test out" a book before committing to it benefits struggling or reluctant readers.

Anticipation responses can be used in any content area with new material, such as a new textbook or a new chapter. Students can browse the subtitles, pictures, and any other material that stands out; read a few paragraphs; and make their inferences, predictions, and connections. In this way, they activate any prior knowledge and provide themselves with a purpose to read.

# PART II

## During-Reading Response

# 3

# Journaling

## Setup for Success

## READING EXPERIENCES IN MY CLASSROOM

There are three types of reading experiences in my classroom: shared reading, small-group or book club reading, and individual reading. I alternate reading experiences (units) with writing units for the first half of the year, because I believe that to learn each of the three modes of writing and to become skilled at reading strategies through shared readings—short stories, poetry, articles, and then a novel—students need to be immersed in each experience. Once the students have become proficient and independent in their reading and writing strategies, I begin to alternate reading workshop and writing workshop days. Figure 3.1 is a chart of my typical academic year, which I have included for reference; however, a yearlong plan for training reader response will work with any curricular plan. I begin my year with a writing unit; therefore, the students begin their reading and journaling independently as homework. Because of this, I begin slowly with response journaling.

## THE READING JOURNAL

Each student needs a two-pocket folder with prong fasteners; I purchase inexpensive folders during preschool sales and distribute them to students, but folders can be added to student supply lists. I advise students that they may want to purchase vinyl folders, which will last all year, rather than paper journals, which will need to be replaced during the year. These become their "Reading Journals." I distribute the Independent Reading Requirements (see Resource B, #1) for students and parents to read, sign, and fasten into the Reading Journals. Each student is also given a "Daily Reading Log" (see Resource B, #2) to include in the Journal.

**Figure 3.1** Sample: Reading-Writing Year Schedule

| Semester 1 | 3 weeks | 3 weeks | 3 weeks | 3 weeks | 3 weeks | 3 weeks |
|---|---|---|---|---|---|---|
| Class Daily | **Writing Workshop**<br>• Informational writing | **Reading Workshop**<br>• Shared reading: Short stories<br>• Strategy lessons | **Writing Workshop**<br>• Persuasive writing | **Reading Workshop**<br>• Drama<br>• Holocaust study | **Reading Workshop**<br>• Shared reading: Novel | **Writing Workshop**<br>• Narrative writing |
| Response | • Response journaling lessons | • Response incorporating focus lessons: Strategies and literary elements | • Continue response using strategies studied | • Poetry response | • Double-entry response | • Author's craft response |
| Homework | • Self-selected independent reading | • Self-selected independent reading | • Self-selected independent reading | • Self-selected Holocaust novel reading | • Shared novel reading | • Self-selected independent reading |

| Semester 2 | 3 weeks—alternating days | 3 weeks—alternating days | 12 weeks—alternating days |
|---|---|---|---|
| Class—Day 1 | **Reading Workshop**<br>• Book clubs | **Reading Workshop**<br>• Memoir reading | **Reading Workshop**<br>• Self-selected independent reading: Nonfiction and fiction |
| Class—Day 2 | **Writing Workshop**<br>• Collaborative writings or poetry writing | • Memoir writing | **Writing Workshop**<br>• Self-selected independent writing: Expository and narrative |
| Response | • Book club response | • Interactive response | • Multigenre and choice response |
| Homework | • Book club reading | • Alternating reading/writing | • Alternating reading/writing |

Students are to read 5 nights per week for at least 25 minutes each night, and they are to write a 5-minute response after each reading in their Journals. On the Daily Logs, they are to document their reading: title, author, genre, amount of time read, and pages read. When they continue reading the same book, they only need to log the time and pages read. If students read any newspaper or magazine articles that week, they need to log them also. In the right-hand column, they will note any focus lesson taught in class, because they are to incorporate the focus lessons into their journal responses whenever appropriate to their reading that week.

Students' Reading Journals each include a 8.5 × 11 inch cardstock "Record of Books Read" so that readers can record when they start and finish a book and rate the book and the reading challenge (see Figure 3.2). Newspapers and magazine articles read are entered on the Daily Log but not the Record of Books Read Record. The reverse side of the Record of Books Read holds a "Genre Chart" divided into 20 genre squares (see Figure 3.3).

**Figure 3.2** Form: Record of Books Read

| RECORD OF BOOKS READ | | | | | | |
|---|---|---|---|---|---|---|
| Book Title | Author | Genre | Date Begun | Date Finished | Rating ☺☻☹ | Difficulty E-JR-C |
| 1. | | | | | | |
| 2. | | | | | | |
| 3. | | | | | | |
| 4. | | | | | | |
| 5. | | | | | | |
| 6. | | | | | | |
| 7. | | | | | | |
| 8. | | | | | | |
| 9. | | | | | | |
| 10. | | | | | | |
| 11. | | | | | | |
| 12. | | | | | | |
| 13. | | | | | | |

**Figure 3.3**   Form: Genre Record

| GENRE RECORD CHART | | | | |
|---|---|---|---|---|
| MYSTERY | HORROR SUSPENSE | INFORMATIONAL | SPORTS | RELATIONSHIPS FAMILY |
| HISTORICAL/WAR | FANTASY | ROMANCE | NOT FITTING IN | POETRY |
| MEMOIR BIOGRAPHY AUTOBIOGRAPHY | SCI-FI/FUTURISTIC | ADVENTURE | SHORT STORY COLLECTIONS | GRAPHIC NOVELS |
| OTHER _____ _____ _____ | CLASSICS | MULTICULTURAL | FOLKTALES | STREET LIFE |

When you complete a book, place a sticker in the appropriate genre box (1 sticker/book).
My goal is _____ books; _____ genres.

Readers write their goals—the numbers of books and genres they aspire to read for the school year—on the bottom of the Genre Chart. When they finish books, they are given star stickers in the appropriate genre box. Readers are not expected to fill all the boxes, and no prize is given out for the most stars since students read books of different lengths, but the stickers make them aware of when it is time to expand their reading. We are looking for variety in reading. I have heard students say, as they put their fourth sticker in a box, "I guess I should try a new genre." Sometimes they ask me for suggestions, and my class library is divided and labeled by genre. Figures 3.4 and 3.5 show examples of one student's Reading Record and Genre Chart.

| Figure 3.4 | Sample: Megan's Reading Record (Midyear) |

### RECORD OF BOOKS READ

| BOOK TITLE | Author | Genre | Date Begun | Date Finished | Rating ☺☺☹ | Dificulty E–JR–C |
|---|---|---|---|---|---|---|
| 1. Girl in Blue | Ann Rinaldi | Historical | 9/4 | 9/19 | ☺ | JR |
| 2. The Staircase | Ann Rinaldi | Historical | 9/22 | 10/3 | ☺ | C |
| 3. A Break with Charity | Ann Rinaldi | Historical | 10/6 | 10/13 | ☺ | JR |
| 4. The Fifth of March | Ann Rinaldi | Historical | 10/14 | 10/17 | ☺ | C |
| 5. Ophelia | Lisa Klein | Romance | 10/21 | 10/30 | ☺ | JR |
| 6. The Wedding | Nicholas Sparks | Romance | 11/5 | ABANDONED | | D — |
| 7. The Secret Garden | F.H. Burnett | Mystery | 11/3 | 11/21 | ☹ | E |
| 8. Summer of my Soldier (German) | Bette Greene | Holocaust | 11/22 | 12/1 | ☹ | JR |
| 9. The Postcard | Beverly Lewis | Not Fitting In | 12/2 | 12/24 | ☺ | JR |
| 10 Sunrise | Karen Kingsbury | Relationships | 12/25 | 1/3 | ☺ | JR |
| 11 A Girl's Guide To Life | Catherine Dee | Informational | 1/5 | 1/9 | ☹ | E |
| 12 | | | | | | |
| 13 | | | | | | |

I find it important for students to keep these records so that, at points during the year, they can self-analyze their reading. Even in the relatively rare case that students lose their Reading Journals, they usually can remember, for the most part, the amount and type of reading they have done just from writing it down and surveying their records as they add information. The readers are now ready to learn the art of response.

| Figure 3.5 | Sample: Megan's Genre Chart (Midyear) |
| --- | --- |

GENRE RECORD CHART

| MYSTERY | HORROR/SUSPENSE | INFORMATIONAL | SPORTS | RELATIONSHIPS |
| --- | --- | --- | --- | --- |
| ★ | ✳ | | | ★ |
| HISTORICAL/WAR ★ ★ ★ ✳ ★ | FANTASY | ROMANCE ★ | NOT FITTING IN ★ | POETRY |
| MEMOIR BIOGRAPHY/ AUTOBIOGRAPHY | SCI-FI FUTURISTIC | ADVENTURE | SHORT STORY COLLECTIONS | GRAPHIC NOVELS |
| OTHER _____ _____ _____ | CLASSICS | MULTICULTURAL | FOLKTALES | STREET LIFE |

When you complete a book, place a sticker in the appropriate genre box (1 sticker/book). My goal is __12__ books; __5__ genres.

# TEACHING DURING-READING RESPONSE

At this point, the students have chosen their books and written anticipation responses (see Chapter 2). I now introduce the concept of daily during-reading responses. I begin with a demonstration for which I use an especially provocative passage from a story or article. I either distribute copies of the passage or place a copy on the overhead projector. I then read it aloud:

> The sun shines cold on a summer's day in the Wonderland of late. The grass has left behind its emerald luster, yet the golden-gray reeds stand at attention beside the winding path, like an army that has lost the battle but retains its dignity. Pebbles scatter over the dry, dusty road, and the ground is beginning to crack as tufts of grass invade the hard path. Lacking traffic, the road slowly blends into the meadow. It has not departed completely, and those who remember can follow the path as it meanders around trees and over brooks. However, all the trees are bare and the brooks merely dry ditches covered by planks of rotted wood. The road winds through the desolate forest until it breaks in two. Slumped at the intersection is a twisted, gnarled tree. Knotholes and deep lines are etched into the trunk, one for each tick of the clock. Above the trunk rests a crown of dark, shiny leaves,

the only greenery in the ghastly un-forest. Various shades of green coat the entire top of the tree, except for one naked branch protruding from the base. This is not the strangest thing, though; resting on the branch is a large cat, popping in and out of reality.

—from "Wonderland Revisited" by Matt Roessing (1993)

To ensure responses, I ask the class who was born in January, February, or March. Students cannot resist; they raise their hands. I ask them for a *question* they might have about the text:

"Is this the Wonderland of *Alice and Wonderland?*

"What battle did the army lose?" (I can see that figurative language has to be discussed.)

"Is the cat going to be a character in the story?"

Next are the spring babies—April and May. They fall for it again. "What is a *prediction* you have?"

"The cat is the Cheshire Cat." (These kids know their stories!)

"Someone is going to come down the path—maybe a very old Alice."

"Maybe a descendant of Alice." (Nice vocabulary.)

The summer births are ready for me; they know what's coming. I may lose some volunteers, but sometimes students feel that they *have* to raise their hands, that they are not showing off. And then there are the friends who rat them out. "Kristen's birthday is July 10!" Additionally, what I am asking seems easy. It's just their opinion. In fact, it seems too easy. I ask them to complete the sentence "I liked the way the *author* . . ."

"set the scene. I can picture it."

"made it sound worn out and sad." (Save this for a lesson on mood.)

"makes up a word: *un-forest.*"

The September and October birthday kids are asked what this passage makes them *think of.*

"The woods behind my house. They are scary."

"My cat. He is constantly disappearing but appears magically at dinnertime."

And the November and December children (who are obvious as being the only ones left) finish the phrase "I *noticed* . . ."

"a simile: 'like an army.'" (Good, someone got it; at least some of them are familiar with similes.)

"an oxymoron: 'sun shines cold.'" (Yay!)

"that this passage describes the setting of the story. It seems like it takes place long after the original story."

I explain that what they have been doing is reader response. As readers of the passage, they responded honestly and in divergent ways; they were all interacting with the text. No responses were "wrong." I further explain that they will be reading their self-selected texts each night and responding in this way in their journals for five minutes.

## AVOIDING RETELLING: RESPONSE STARTERS

Even though we go through this exercise, I have found that the greatest problem with students' responses at the beginning of the year is that adolescents write summaries instead of reflections. They were proficient with our sample for two reasons: I led the responses, and they were aware that we all read the same passage. When they read independently, however, students often use up their five-minute response time retelling their reading. I have found that in some cases, beginning response works better if students feel they are writing letters. I model this form of response with a book I read. I explain that another teacher and I purchased copies of the same book, *Elsewhere* by Gabrielle Zevin, and we decided to read the novel at the same time and write responses to each other. I show them examples of some of my first responses:

---

Dear Mrs. B,

**Response 1—My Anticipation Response:**

Thank you for finding *Elsewhere* for us to read together. Maybe this is the "Elsewhere" that Jonas escaped to at the end of *The Giver*. If not, it sounds like it's on the same track. I like books that have a different perspective, like *The Lovely Bones* and *The Five People You'll Meet in Heaven*. From the cover blurb, this book seems somewhat like those. I think it will be fantasy. I wonder why there is a snow globe on the cover . . .

**Response 2—"Prologue"**

I couldn't believe the dog was the narrator of the first chapter. Were you as surprised as I was? I had no clue until the dead giveaway (the chewing), and then I had to go back to reread it to see if it all fit together. I might have seen it coming, but it was so unusual and really violated my expectations. It also gave me some things to think about. However, even though it was clever, I'm glad the author only used that convention for the first chapter.

**Response 3—"At Sea"**

A boat? I wonder why the author used that setting.

I was surprised that Liz didn't know she was dead. What I found interesting was that she was so sure she is having a dream. I have never had a dream where I knew I was dreaming.

This reminds me of a conversation I had with Mrs. Pitts about college roommates and how that is usually the biggest problem with freshman year of college, but Liz seems to have accepted her roommate being a complete stranger even before she came up with the dream theory.

*(Continued)*

(Continued)

**Response 4—"Curtis Jest"**

Boy, for teens to be stuck on a ship with senior citizens must be their worst nightmare, but so far Liz hasn't said anything about that. However, I can just *hear* Myra with her New York accent; my niece Karen has the "typical" New York accent. Will Curtis, the rock star, become an important character? Somehow I doubt it, but the author *is* tying in events from Liz's life. Do you think that this ship centers somehow on Liz's life and there are other ships with other people?

**Response 5—"Curtis Jest" continued**

I guess the ship is a symbol that she is traveling somewhere, but ships are not *my* favorite method of travel!

I must say that this present-tense writing is driving me crazy; I don't like it when stories are in present tense—especially third-person stories. I would have written this in past tense.

**Response 6—"In Memory of . . ."**

When Thandi says, "Girl, you are in underline{denial}," it reminded me of an old "Denial is not a river in Egypt," saying, and then I realized that they are on the *S.S. Nile!* Coincidence?

I loved the "You can't help but be on time for NOW" comment; I love playing with words (and time). Liz observing her own funeral reminded me of *Huck Finn*. I am guessing that she will want to view more of earth.

---

I place a copy of this first-week letter to Mrs. B on the projector. As I read my six responses, I give any necessary background information; however, the class can appreciate that, even without knowing the plot, they can follow my responses and see that I am reading and interacting with the book. Next I distribute paper copies of this "journal," asking the students to highlight sentence stems. After a few minutes, I ask for volunteers, and when they have shared all the stems they found, I show a copy on the overhead with the response words in bolded red or underlined.

*Anticipation Response:*

Thank you for finding *Elsewhere* for us to read together. Maybe this is the "Elsewhere" that Jonas escaped to at the end of *The Giver.* If not, **it sounds like** it's on the same track. **I like** books that have a different perspective, like *The Lovely Bones* and *The Five People You'll Meet in Heaven.* From the cover blurb, **this book seems** somewhat like those. **I think** it will be fantasy. **I wonder** why there is a snow globe on the cover . . .

*"Prologue"*

**I couldn't believe** the dog was the narrator of the first chapter. Were you as surprised as I was? **I had no clue** until the dead giveaway (the chewing), and then **I had to go back to reread** it to see if it all fit together. I might have seen it coming, but it was so unusual and really **violated my expectations. It also gave** me some things to think about. However, even though it was clever, **I'm glad** the author only used that convention for the first chapter.

*"At Sea"*

A boat? **I wonder** why the author used that setting.

**I was surprised** that Liz didn't know she was dead. What **I found interesting** was that she was so sure she is having a dream. I have never had a dream where I knew I was dreaming.

**This reminds me** of a conversation I had with Mrs. Pitts about college roommates and how that is usually the biggest problem with freshman year of college, but Liz seems to have accepted her roommate being a complete stranger even before she came up with the dream theory.

*"Curtis Jest"*

Boy, for teens to be stuck on a ship with senior citizens must be their worst nightmare, but so far Liz hasn't said anything about that. However, **I can just** *hear* Myra with her New York accent; my niece Karen has the "typical" New York accent. **Will** Curtis, the rock star, become an important character? Somehow **I doubt** it, but the author *is* tying in events from Liz's life. **Do you think** that this ship centers somehow on Liz's life and there are other ships with other people?

**I guess** the ship is a symbol that she is traveling somewhere, but ships are not *my* favorite method of travel!

I must say that this present-tense writing is driving me crazy; **I don't like it** when stories are in present tense—especially third-person stories. I would have written this in past tense.

*"In Memory of . . ."*

When Thandi says, "Girl, you are in <u>denial</u>," **it reminded me** of an old "Denial is not a river in Egypt," saying, and then **I realized** that they are on the *S.S. Nile!* Coincidence?

**I loved** the "You can't help but be on time for NOW," comment; **I love** playing with words (and time).

Liz observing her own funeral **reminded me** of *Huck Finn.* **I am guessing** that she will want to view more of earth.

I then hand out a list of Response Starters (see Resource B, #3) to add to their Reading Journals, and we examine them. We discuss some of the stems, and students are encouraged to suggest others to add to the list. Since I have not yet taught reading strategies, we are not pointing out that "I am guessing" is a prediction and "reminded me of *Huck Finn*" is text-to-text connection; if they do bring those terms into the conversation, then I become aware of what they have learned in previous classes and can adjust my future lessons accordingly.

As practice, I distribute a short story or article to read, text that most can finish in about 20–25 minutes. If the students have greatly divergent reading levels and paces, I may hand out a few different stories with which I am familiar. After 25 minutes, I request that they stop reading, write a response, and continue writing until I notify them to stop. I time them and advise that they wrap up their responses at five minutes. Afterwards, they look at their writing—a "representative" five-minute response; most are surprised at how much they can write in five minutes. This exercise discourages two-sentence responses in their weekly journals. It also serves as an adaptation, because proficient reader-writers can write more in five minutes than struggling reader-writers. After this exercise I—and they—know how much can be expected from them. I ask students to store this sample in one of the folder pockets for now as a gauge for themselves and for me. I repeat this exercise from time to time as a reminder because I do not want them actually sitting with a clock when they respond.

A second reason for this exercise is to encourage students to go back and consider the stems they used. They can check off or add to the Response Starters list in their journals. At various times during the year, students have contributed additional Response Starters, such as "What caught my attention . . . ," "The plot took a surprise turn when . . . ," "I was confused by/when . . . ," and "A different way I can relate to. . . ." I advise them that they do not have to look at the Response Starters list before or when they write—only if they have trouble getting started or find themselves summarizing, rather than responding; they are to refer to the list only *when* and *if* needed. Again, it is scaffolding that they can take down at any point.

In this example, Kaitlyn begins her response to Chapter 4 of *Encyclopedia Brown Shows the Way*, by Donald J. Sobol, which I used as the guided practice:

> I wonder why this boy went to this show with his friend even though he didn't really want to. I must say that I can relate to him because I would be afraid also because I become scared easily and turn the movie into reality, while Taylor reflected: I think this story is going to end up that there is just a person behind the light. . . . I think he [the author] gives good descriptions of the boys, like when he said, "Charlie shot into the air as if he were practicing to be a human cannonball." I began to think of the *Scooby-Doo* TV show.

## INDEPENDENT READING RESPONSE

Readers are now ready to begin reading and responding independently as homework while we begin a writing unit in class. They will continue to do so as we work on reading strategy and more response lessons in class by means of short, shared readings—short stories, poetry, and articles. During the week, I also fit in some independent reading and response time after our scheduled lesson. At this point, each student's Reading Journal should contain Independent Reading Requirements, Record of Books Read/Genre Chart, Daily Reading Log, Response Starters, and about ten pieces of composition paper fastened in the center section in that order. Their journals also contain a "Reading Interests" chart on which readers can list their general interests, favorite authors, and favorite genres so that I can recommend books to them (Resources B, #4); this form includes a "Book Pass: Books for Future Reading" chart on which readers can record books that other readers have recommended or books from book talks or book passes that have aroused their interest.

I photocopy these papers and any other reading handouts onto colored paper (blue) so that they stand out from the student-generated papers and are easy to locate. A week or two later, after students are familiar with the requirements and I have taught abandonment responses, students replace the Independent Reading Requirements handout with the "Starting to Finishing a Book" guidelines in Figure 3.6.

| **Figure 3.6** | Guidelines: Starting to Finishing a Book |
|---|---|

### When You *Begin* a Book

1. Enter start date, title, author, and genre on your **Record of Books Read**.

2. Look at the front and back covers and inside flaps (of hardbacks) and read the first few pages of your book. Write an **anticipation response**, including "How I chose this book" as your first entry.

### While You *Read* a Book

1. Fill out your **Log** daily with pages and time every time you read in class (C) or at home.

2. Read for 25 minutes at home, even when we have independent reading time in class.

3. After (or while) you read, respond for five minutes in your **Journal.** Integrate our focus lessons whenever applicable.

### If You *Abandon* a Book

1. Write "Abandoned" and the date on your **Record of Books Read.**

2. Write a response about why you abandoned the book.

### After You *Finish* a Book

1. Write a final response for the book as a whole, evaluating it based on whatever criteria you think important. Look over your journal entries and comment on your reading of, and responses to, the book.

2. Enter date finished, rating, and reading level on the **Record of Books Read**.

3. Get a star sticker for your **Genre Chart**.

4. Return the book to the library, if applicable. If it's from our class library, put the card back in the pocket and put the book back on the appropriate genre shelf.

5. You may sign up for extra-credit book talk or write a recommendation in the eBoard Book Blog or write a review for our Recommendations binder in our library.

---

### Extra-Credit Book Talks

1. Hand in an outline showing that you prepared your presentation. (You can refer to it during your talk.)

2. Show the book and have a good lead in to your talk (attention-grabber).

3. Tell about the following:

    1. Title

    2. Author

    3. Genre

    4. Setting: Time and place

    5. Main characters and their characteristics

    6. Plot—Conflict—Climax (unless it would ruin the book for future readers)

    7. Favorite part: You can read your favorite scene or description.

    8. Author's style: You can read an example.

    9. Comparison to another novel, author, movie, or TV show

    10. Recommendation: Yes or no, why, and for what type of reader

4. Practice and demonstrate good public speaking techniques—volume, pace, eye contact, posture.

All journals are set up the same way so that students can first look at the starting-to-finishing guidelines until the procedures become second nature, and the Response Starters are next to their journaling pages. This order benefits me because I can look at their Reading Record to see what book they are currently reading, then scan their Daily Log to ascertain their reading pattern for the week, and last turn to their journal pages to read their entries. My students are now ready to begin to read and respond. Their practice five-minute response is in the pocket to remind them and me of roughly the type of response I can expect.

Many mimic my letters to Mrs. B., writing to me or to friends. They also may write to the author. These are not letters that they actually mail because they are responses only to one night's reading. However, when we write after-reading responses (see Chapter 9), I may encourage students to write a letter and send it to an author. They also may choose to write a response as a character in their novel. Amanda did it all:

> Walter Dean Myers,
>
> I am writing this letter to inform you that your book, Monster, is incredible. I am enjoying reading it, and I like how you express the characters' feelings so well. I like how Steven Harmon is young, and you tell about young life that I can relate to. I feel very bad for Steven. I think you should keep on writing your books because how detailed they are. I enjoyed reading the script—how it was set up, like a real movie script with camera angles. I liked the different fonts in the book. It made me feel like I was at the court with Steven when I read. Thank you for making such an enjoyable book.
>
> Your fan, Amanda

> Dear my friend Colleen,
>
> I strongly suggest you read the book I am reading. I like how the narrator really tells you what is happening. I am halfway into this book, and I feel like I was there, seeing every moment in Steve's horrible life. I feel really sad while reading this book because it is about a boy who is in jail. Monster is one of the best books I have ever read because you feel like you know the characters. If you enjoy reading realistic fiction, this is truly the one for you.
>
> Your friend Amanda

Amanda's responses do not contain a lot of analysis at this time, but she is only beginning her training. She has some nice stems, such as "I like how," "I feel," "It made me feel like," and "because" statements, and she classifies the genre.

In my favorite response, Amanda writes *as* the protagonist, describing his feelings about going to court and living as part of a prison community:

> *Monster* Response #6:
>
> Tonite I did something different while I was reading. I put myself in the main character's shoes. I felt as if no one cared about me. I also was scared about if I would lose the trial or win it. I thought about what I had done and wondered why did I do it. This story really makes me think, If I was in Steven's shoes, how would I react? I thought about it and wrote down a journal entry as Steven:

Dear Diary,

Today was harsh. They called me up as I was getting ready for court. I thought I was getting in more trouble, but it was just one of my friends at the jail saying "Good luck." I was nervous, impatient to find out the results of my case. As I entered the courtroom, my heart dropped of shock. During court, I was scared to talk in front of a lot of people. Then, as the lights went out that night, I was scared that it might have been my turn to get beat up.

Amanda (Steven's shoes)

I use Amanda's examples to show my classes some of the choices they have, even at this preliminary point. By modeling, I find that those who would not otherwise attempt the assignment copy the example and the more creative or adventurous use models as a jumping-off point. The more samples shared, the better the tentative students become.

I can discover any problems at the beginning of the year. In fact, I find that often I have to repeat the 30-minute reading-responding exercise, using a short text or even the students' independent reading books, after the first Reading Journals have been submitted. After a duplication lesson, I usually only have a few students who are retelling stories rather than responding to them. In those few cases, I may give them a form with one or two general Response Starters, such as "I wonder . . . " and "I liked the way the author . . . ," per night for the next week and then ask them to write Response Starters themselves on a form for another week, weaning them slowly. By the third or fourth week, all of my students are reflecting on their reading, even though some still include summarization.

I emphasize that responses can be written after a reading session. Responding is not to interrupt their reading, unless they prefer to read and jot. Reflective reading does not have to interfere with aesthetic reading.

## ABANDONMENT RESPONSE

I have a closet bursting with clothing that I don't wear: fat clothes, skinny clothes, out-of-style clothes (bell bottoms did come back, but hot pink hasn't—yet). Sometimes it is just time to let go. At times, students legitimately need to abandon a book, even after having gone through all the right steps when choosing it. Even though anticipation responses reduce the frequency of abandonment, sometimes students ask me if they are "allowed" to stop reading a book. Of course, since this is choice reading, I tell them that they are.

To prepare them for this situation, I ask my classes to brainstorm reasons why they would wish to abandon a book. But first we discuss how much time a reader needs to give a book before considering abandonment; they usually come up with "at least three to four chapters." They list reasons they have stopped reading books in the past:

I didn't like the characters—their personalities or how they handled situations.

The plot became too confusing to follow, or the plot was too predictable.

There were too many characters to follow.

The setting, either place or time period, was too unfamiliar for me to comprehend or picture what was going on.

The author's style became tedious or didn't fit the topic.

I found that, even though I liked the author's style, the topic actually did not interest me as much as I thought it would.

The book was too long, and I found other books that I couldn't wait to begin.

I got bored with the topic or style after a while; it was just too much.

The book just did not fulfill the promise of the covers and the first few pages.

The shift in perspective between characters was too confusing.

I like horror, but the descriptions were just too disgusting.

I talk about a book I abandoned for some of those reasons and write a response on the board:

> I was reading *Ella Minnow Pea.* The book was recommended by a reading buddy, and the premise, the town eliminating letters one at a time, was intriguing. I looked at the covers, read the first few pages, and liked the author's style. However, the book was a series of letters, not my favorite **genre**, and the idea became **repetitive** even though it was amusing. I think that if **another book** I really was waiting to read hadn't become available right then, I may have finished the book, and I might still go back to it at a later date.

The students then choose an abandonment experience from the past, talk about it with a partner to revive memories, and practice writing about it for five minutes. An abandonment response becomes part of their reading regimen, when applicable, because it is a response to reading on the day they decide to abandon the book. This exercise makes them think about why they are not enjoying the book and, possibly, how they could have avoided that situation. In other words, did they read the book just because it was sitting on a table at home and they needed a book that day, just because a friend had enjoyed it, or because it was a "thin" book? Through their analyses, they come to such conclusions as "a thick book is only long if you are not enjoying it" and "a thin book can be too long."

Hollie loved one novel by author Jodi Picoult but found herself to be less engaged by the length and topic of another:

> I am abandoning my book *Nineteen Minutes* because I just can't get into the book. I like to be able to sit down and enjoy a book, not have to reread or try to comprehend everything that happens and [figure out] who is talking. Another thing is at night when I want to lay down and read an interesting book, I can't because it [the novel] is about shooting, and I have to think a lot. The reason I picked it is because I liked the book *My Sister's Keeper,* but this book is just taking too long.

Alyssa seemed more disappointed in herself than her book:

> Unfortunately, this is an abandonment response. A goal I had for this year was to not abandon any book that I start. I have failed! *Dragon's Breath* was a huge disappointment. I abandoned this book because it was uninteresting to me. There were too many characters popping up all the time. I did not think it was well-written

at all. *Frog Princess* was amazing, but the sequel could not match it. I usually do think that sequels are not as good as the original. I may pick up *Dragon's Breath* in the summer again . . . I really wanted to find out what happens to Haywood. I think that if the author left out extra words and minor characters and details, then the book would be just as good as the first. It was like every page there is a new character. It was also a little too fantasy for me. I enjoy fantasy but it made the book seem too unreal. *Dragon's Breath* is also below my reading level.

When she originally chose the book, Alyssa wrote quite an extensive anticipation response, where she noted,

I have begun to read *Dragon's Breath* by E. D. Baker. I chose to read this book because it is the sequel to *The Frog Princess.* I really enjoyed *Frog Princess* so hopefully this book will be even better. I like to read books about dragons because I read the *Eragon* series and I really enjoyed them.

She further observed and explained why "the summary on the back was interesting to me. . . ." However, there were hints that she might not be as pleased with this book as she hoped when she read over the first few pages and commented, "After reading the first few pages I started to get annoyed at Aunt Grassina. . . . Otherwise the book is okay."

Three days later, within her daily response, Alyssa wrote,

The crab is the same one that Eadric and Emma were chasing during the storm. I thought that was unnecessary because we do not need all of these extra characters. There is too much going on right now in the book. . . . *The Frog Princess* really grabbed my attention and this book is not. . . . I am just starting out so hopefully it will get better over time.

Eight days after, having read to page 142, Alyssa abandoned the novel and analyzed the reasons in her abandonment response. I cannot say she didn't give the book a fighting chance. In fact, I responded to her comment that she "failed," writing, "The book may have failed you."

## ADAPTATIONS

A variety of adaptations can be made for struggling or reluctant readers and writers when journaling. Even though the more time adolescents spend reading, the better readers they become, we must be realistic and realize that at the beginning, our goal is to hook the embryonic reader. I use in-class independent reading time as "extra," nonresponse time in addition to their half-hour homework reading so that students can have almost a full hour of reading a day whenever possible. However, as an

**Photo 3.1** Author Lesley Roessing confers with students Andrew and Hei

adaptation for reluctant readers who refuse to read at home, teachers may need to regard the in-class independent reading as homework reading time. Most of our students carry their books with them so that if there is extra time in another class or during our team enrichment period (a study or extra-help period for those students who do not have scheduled activities), they can read. Our homeroom and content area teachers have come to expect to see students reading during any "extra" time.

Another adaptation for struggling readers is to ensure that I demonstrate a variety of response examples. Also, I give them an example to keep in their journals; it can be photocopied onto the reverse side of their Response Starters sheet. I ensure that the model meets the abilities of the students who are using it. As mentioned above, the five-minute response practice demonstrates that all students are able to write varied amounts in five minutes and differentiates expectations.

# 4

# Double-Entry Journaling and Sticky Notes

I begin my students' path towards independence with shared, or whole-class, readings. Together we start with short stories, poetry, and informational articles—texts that we can read during class time and discuss together. Through these texts, I teach literary devices, reading strategies, and response-journaling techniques. I think that it is vital that I introduce to the whole class and we practice together. Shared texts also give us a common experience to which we can refer during the year.

Some believe that read-alouds should serve as the only shared readings, but students need to engage with complete works, even if short, to provide scaffolding that stays in place. And they need to work on them together. My students remember most of our short stories, which we read as shared texts, even late in the year, making reference to characters such as Squeaky from "Raymond's Run" or Laurie from "Charles." However, they rarely refer back to my read-alouds. Because we have worked with the shared texts for a few days, we can build on to them, and the characters become old friends.

After we read one short story or article to learn or review each reading strategy and literary element, we read a novel together to complete our literary study before moving on to book club reading. During this time, I concentrate on linking reading response to our reading strategy lessons.

## DOUBLE-ENTRY JOURNALING

Free-response journaling (see Chapter 3) is a constructive initiation to reader response technique, but it serves only as the groundwork as we teach our students, on their way to becoming independent readers, to make their responses more meaningful. In many cases, I want my students to learn to focus their responses on actual text—a quote, a description, a figure of speech, a character, an event, a symbol—so that they become more aware of their interactions and more actively engaged with the text. This gives the reader Rosenblatt's "verbal basis" for interpretation. In other words, students have textual references to back up their responses. Using free response during the first weeks of school, Brittany journals her response to that day's reading of *Dangerously Alice:*

> This reminds me when our family has a big Thanksgiving dinner. And we cook a big turkey and everyone brings something. And when we are done eating we tell stories and look at pictures. Their family Thanksgiving reminds me of ours. And their family had a fun time and laughed a lot.

I would like to know, and would like Brittany to reflect on, what evidence in the text made her think that Alice's family was so much like hers and whether it said that they were having fun or if she only assumed that, based on her comparison.

The most effective way to train this skill is the double-entry journal. A double-entry journal allows students to record their thoughts on text or text features as they read. In the left column, which I label "From the BOOK," the reader copies text or jots a plot event, the name of a character, a setting description, some dialogue, etc. In the right column, marked "From Your BRAIN," the reader writes a reaction or response. These two columns can also be identified as "Quotes" and "Notes" or "It Says" and "I Say," as well as a variety of other titles. I prefer the "book" and "brain" nomenclature because the students can tell exactly where the information in each column is to come from and that it does not always have to be a quote but can be a concept. Double-entry journals show the teacher what the student thinks is important in the text.

As with all journaling techniques, I use a gradual release model: I demonstrate and then have students work together in class on a short reading, usually a poem or an interesting article, as guided practice. Last, I require students to list this as a focus lesson in their Logs to remind them to practice the journaling approach individually with their independent reading a few times during the week. I give them a Double-Entry Response Journal form to add to their journals.

## STRATEGY RESPONSES

For my focus lesson, I first use the example of a popular nursery rhyme, "Jack and Jill," and continue using the same nursery rhyme as an introduction to double-entry responses using reading strategies. For example, if I am teaching or reviewing the reading strategy "Asking questions of the text," I place this on the overhead projector:

> Jack and Jill went up the hill,
>
> To fetch a pail of water.
>
> Jack fell down and broke his crown,
>
> And Jill came tumbling after.

I then uncover my double entry:

| From the BOOK | From Your BRAIN |
| --- | --- |
| "Jack and Jill went . . . to fetch . . . water." | When did this take place? Before running water? Or was the family too poor to afford water? |

**Figure 4.1**    Double-Entry Response Journal—General

| Date _____    Title _____    Pages _____ to _____ |||
|---|---|---|
| **Double-Entry Response Journal** |||
| From the **BOOK** (facts, quotes) | From Your **BRAIN** (thoughts, reactions, opinions) | Page |
| 1. | | _____ |
| | | |
| | | |
| | | |
| | | |
| 2. | | _____ |
| | | |
| | | |
| | | |
| | | |
| 3. | | _____ |
| | | |
| | | |
| | | |
| | | |
| 4. | | _____ |
| | | |
| | | |
| | | |
| | | |

At that point, I can add more questions or invite students to add their questions. I point out that this format lets them, and me, see exactly what text provokes the question. When reading longer literary works, they may want or need to refer back to the text when they find the answer. I have read many response journals from other teachers where the students only make a list of questions; the teacher is not aware of the source of the questions. Writing down the text lets the teacher see that connection, and it makes the questions more profound as the readers think about them, comprising *a response to the text*. Many students have said that once they copy the words from the text, they can see that they actually do not have a question or that their question is not important to understanding the writing.

I may then continue with a longer read-aloud, stopping and asking questions as I read. To save time, I will type the text that I will question on the left side of a transparency, uncovering it and adding my questions to the right side as I read. This is not spontaneous. As with all focus lessons, the teacher should prepare and practice the lesson before presenting.

The students next attempt a guided practice, using a short text and a divided piece of composition paper, working in pairs or individually. In small groups, they compare their entries. In one class, I distributed a *National Geographic Kids News* article on the ancient Olympics for practice. The students wrote questions such as these:

| From the BOOK | From Your BRAIN |
| --- | --- |
| 1. "Athens is the birthplace of the Olympics. . . . The games got their name from Olympia, the Greek city where they took place." | 1. I'm confused. If the games took place in Olympia, why is Athens their "birthplace"? |
| 2. "The ancient Olympics existed until 393 CE." | 2. Why did the Olympics stop until 1896, the first modern Olympics (paragraph 1)? |

As homework, the students are to apply this technique to their reading, and I give them a Double-Entry Journal—Questioning to add to their Reading Journals (see Resource B, # 5). For certain classes, I include a space for a short summary at the top of the form. I do this for two reasons. First, I have found that if readers don't have a space for summary, they feel they must share the events of the book with me and write a retelling within or instead of their responses; they still do not appreciate that I can follow their comments without having read their book. Second, summarizing is a good strategy in itself, and the few lines allotted force students to choose only the most important details. If we are reading a shared novel, they can look back for certain information and locate the chapters that contain it, or they can read ahead and remember not to divulge "future" plot events in class. I encourage readers to bullet-point plot events, rather than writing a paragraph, so that they keep their summary and their responses separate.

The next day, I continue the practice of questioning, this time focusing on *types* of questions. Using the "Jack and Jill" transparency from the previous day, the students categorize their questions. "When?" is a question about setting, while "What's a 'crown'?" is a vocabulary question.

The class next practices with "Casey at the Bat" by Ernest Thayer, a narrative poem I use as a touchstone text multiple times during the year because of its length, high interest, and versatility. I reduce the size of the poem when typing or photocopying so that it fits on approximately the left 50 percent of the handout. To save time, we highlight the text we would include on the left side of our double-entry journal and write on the right side of the paper as if it were our journals. My students collectively generated a list of questions, which they grouped and categorized (see Figure 4.2).

If teachers want students to identify the type of question in their journals, an additional column can be added to the form, but I feel that it is sufficient to make them

| Figure 4.2 | "Casey at the Bat"—Strategy: Questioning |
| --- | --- |

Types of Questions

**About Plot**

Will Casey get to bat?

Why are Flynn and Jimmy Blake not expected to get Casey to bat?

Will Casey's team win?

Why was everyone so nervous? Was this a championship?

Why did some people leave?

Why did Casey let the first two throws go by?

**About Vocabulary**

*patrons?*

*pall-like?*

*hoo doo?* Is it slang? What time period?

Why would you call someone a *cake?*

**About Characters**

Why were most of the patrons so hopeful? What did they know?

Why was Blake despised? And by whom?

What was Casey's record?

Why was Casey so at ease and proud?

**About Format (Genre)**

Is this story fictional or true?

When was it written?

Why was it written?

Would I react differently if it were a news column?

**About Comprehension**

Mudville *nine*—baseball team?

4 to 2: Who is winning?

Did Cooney really die?

Where are the sun shining and bands playing?

aware of the different questions to explore. Later, as I teach readers to go deeper and respond to questions, we may leave the double-entry journal format and add additional columns such as "Answer," "Where Found," and even "How Found" (see Resource B, #6).

The double-entry form can easily be revised for each reading strategy and for finer distinctions within any strategy. Over the next few weeks, I teach or review reading strategies (Resource B, #7) using individual short stories or articles. I thoroughly exploit "Jack and Jill" as demonstrations for journaling (see Figure 4.3).

**Figure 4.3**  Sample: "Jack and Jill" Double-Entry

*Jack and Jill went up the hill,*
*To fetch a pail of water.*
*Jack fell down and broke his crown,*
*And Jill came tumbling after.*

**Questions About Text**

Jack and Jill went to fetch a pail of water.

When did this take place? Before people had running water?

**Connection: Text to Self**

Jill came tumbling after.

My sister was seven years older, and I was always following her around. If she got in trouble, I got in trouble.

**Connection: Text to Text**

Humpty Dumpty, Little Miss Muffet, Rockabye Baby . . .

Those nursery rhyme characters lived unhappy lives, not what one would expect in a *nursery* rhyme.

**Connection: Text to World**

Jack fell down . . . and Jill came tumbling after.

This could be an analogy of the United States and Britain and the Iraq war. If the United States "falls down," Britain will follow since it was the country that supported our involvement.

**Interesting Quote**

"broke his crown"

I thought that heads were really hard. How does one break his head? Why is the top of the head called a *crown*? Which came first—the head *crown* or the hat *crown*?

**Picture in My Mind (Visualization)**

Jack and Jill went up the hill to fetch water.

**Setting**

The hill

It must have been a pretty high hill if Jack broke his head falling down it. You would think that a well would not be at the top of a hill.

**Inference**

Up a hill to fetch water

Maybe the water was on the *other* side of the hill.

Each time, I relabel the right-hand column ("From the BRAIN") on the Double-Entry Journal for the appropriate type of response: determining importance, making connections, making inferences and predictions, and sketching visualizations.

After I have taught reading strategies, I add a third column to the journal pages for the readers to identify and, therefore, reflect upon the types of strategies they are using in their reading and responses. This third column is introduced when I focus on the strategy of making connections. As the students become adept at making connections, I then ask them to analyze the types of connections made. In the new third column, they classify the connection, the most customary connection being text-to-self, text-to-text, or text-to-world (see Resource B, #8). I customarily teach one reading strategy and one literary element with each shared text. Double-entry journals can also be used for responses to literary elements within a text (see Resource B, #9). This form can be easily modified for any lesson being taught.

I do not expect students to respond using one particular reading strategy every night of the week we are working with it; that would be too unnatural. There are only so many questions, connections, visualizations, and so forth that one reader can have in five readings. The double-entry response pages each have room for three responses. One section can be used for the in-class guided practice, and the other two can be used during the week for independent reading when appropriate. As they learn the double-entry technique, students can record other daily responses as they have been doing.

## PUTTING IT ALL TOGETHER

Finally, as readers advance to utilizing all strategies, double-entry journals can cause them to reflect about which strategies they are employing. After we have completed our initial study or review of reading strategies, I release control and substitute a form that encourages readers to identify the strategies they are using in their responses (see Resource B, #10).

To enable the students to integrate all they have learned so far, I use Mark Vinz's poem "What I Remember About the 6th Grade," because sixth grade is a common experience my eighth graders and I share. I put the poem on the overhead projector and give out copies. I read the poem aloud, and we all respond. My students either highlight or identify the text considered, responding on their papers where I again have left the right side blank. Then I highlight my diverse responses—inferences, connections, and questions—in different colors on my transparency. We compare responses and discuss strategies used. I want to reiterate the point I require the readers to try this technique so that they learn response. Over the year, I will gradually loosen control as readers master, then choose, the most appropriate response techniques for themselves and their reading.

---

**What I Remember About the 6th Grade**

We lost the school softball championship
when that four-eyed kid popped out
with the bases loaded. We did *win the*
*spelling bee,* though. *Weird Charlie* said          *There's one in every class.*
It was because we had the *ugliest girls.*          *Stereotyping: Smart girls are ugly.*

*(Continued)*

---

(Continued)

The Scarlet Tanager edged out the Wood Duck
in our balloting for the *State Bird*                *What is our state bird?*
because *the girls* liked red and *organized.*        *This reminds me of Liddy.*
I voted for the Bluejay or maybe the Loon.
Weird Charlie voted for the Crow.

The teacher nearly got knocked cold when
a big picture of George Washington or somebody
fell off the wall and conked her on the head.
Most of the girls cried. Most of the boys
laughed, especially Weird Charlie.

Once a month or so they'd herd us
to the basement for *atomic bomb drills*             *'50s? Now it's "Stranger Danger"*
                                                     *and hurricane drills.*
and films of houses exploding in firestorms.
When it came to the Nuclear Age,
even Weird Charlie kept his mouth shut.

We have finished working with short stories and now put it all together as we read a shared novel both in class and as homework, replacing the nightly independent reading for the time being. As the next step, I assign a double-entry journal response on one of the homework chapters. Figure 4.4 shows a sample of such a journal response. The next day, I show them a transparency of three of my responses to the same chapter. This gives the readers a chance to compare, confirm that they did it "right," and note what we each found vital enough for comment as they compare their responses with others. This exercise usually boosts their confidence as they see that everyone has different comments and that all are valid and interesting. Some responses model deeper, interpretive thinking. This type of journaling is done for at least two-thirds of the novel-reading time, with readers focusing on what *they* feel is important.

Besides facilitating readers' awareness of what they notice about a text, double-entry journals also help readers discern the strategies they employ. An added bonus, no less important, is that readers are coming to class with something in hand and in mind to discuss. Even the shyer adolescents, who never volunteer discussion points, seem comfortable reading something they have written the night before. They almost look as if writing has magically appeared in their journals and they are reading it on behalf of the author. If someone corrects an assertion, *Well, hey, it was on my paper; I was just reading it.* Writing down ideas also gives students chances to test them before contributing to a class discussion. Journaling makes class discussions richer, since students most likely have gone in divergent directions, many times in response to the same quote or event or character. Previously, when someone began a discussion, I found that most students just followed that student's lead. Most importantly, they all have the *textual evidence* on which they based their comments in the left column. Many times, this leads the class to return to the text to check the context of responses.

**Figure 4.4**   Sample: Cindy's *Haroun* Double-Entry Journal

Summary: The Khalifa family lives in a very sad town while Rashid tells stories. Mrs. Khalifa runs off with Mr. Sengupta at exactly 11 o'clock. Now, their son, Haroun, only has an attention spand of 11 minutes. When Haroun repeates an insulting thing that Mr. Sengupta said, Rashid can't tell any other story.

| From **BOOK:**<br>Character, Setting, Event, Quote | From **BRAIN:**<br>Your personal response, inference, questions | Page |
|---|---|---|
| 1. The poor lived in tumbledown shacks made of old cardboard boxes and plastic sheeting, and these shacks were glued together by despair. | I don't see much of that around here, but once, when I went to Philadephia and saw poor people everywhere. There were people sleeping on the sidewalks, fidgiting because of all the bugs. I saw a homeless shelter and it amazed me at how many people were there. | 18 |
| 2. "What's the use of stories that aren't even true?" - Mr. Sengupta | Stories that aren't true give you a chance to go places. To places that nobody else has been. True stories have an ending that everyone always knows. True stories can't be created or from someone's wildest imagination. Fiction is a work of art that isn't just someone else's life. | 20 |
| 3. Haroun wanted to get those words back, to pull them out of his father's ears and shove them back into his own mouth. | If Haroun didn't believe it when Mr. Sengupta said it, then why did he say it? How could he let something like that slip out? A lot of people say things that they wish they didn't, but why is he taking so long to take it back. | 22 |

# GOING DEEPER: USING STICKY NOTES

Using sticky notes and responding to those notes is a more reflective response phase. The goal of using sticky-note response is to guide readers to probe more deeply and to respond on a more meaningful level. At this point, I want students to consider the reasoning behind their questions, connections, visualizations, and inferences.

We have all seen the connection made to a character who has a dog. Stacey gleefully writes in her journal, "Johnny is given a dog (p. 43). → *I have a dog. Her name is Buttons.*" [Connection: Text to Self]. Never mind that this is not a five-minute response; it is purposeless. I need to take Stacey to the point where she writes about what effect having a dog has on her comprehension of the story. Does having her own dog make Stacey more sympathetic to circumstances in her novel? Does she realize what a responsibility having a dog will be for the character and how that responsibility may affect his situation? Does her experience with a dog make her predict that the character will bond with his pet and finally have some companionship in his rather lonely life?

A new character is introduced. Billy writes, "Who is Kathleen? Will she meet Greg? Will she like Greg?" I want to know, and I want Billy to reflect on, what prompts his questions. Does it matter if Kathleen meets Greg? If so, how might this change the plot, or will it? If she likes Greg, does this alter the conflict? What happens if Greg ignores her? We want our readers not only to comprehend text but to comprehend it on more meaningful levels.

To reach this goal, I ask students to use sticky notes as they read and post them in the text where they have a question, an inference, a prediction, a visualization. They are not to mark the strategies on the sticky note but to jot their actual question, prediction, and so forth on the note. This prevents them from having to interrupt their reading for more than a minute, and it allows for further interaction with the text. I distribute a new type of journal sheet (see Resource B, #11). When they finish their reading session, they choose two or three sticky notes, stick them on the left side of the journal page, and then explore the motivation for their comments—for example, they observe what triggered an inference and its significance to the reading. They then write a response *to their sticky note* on the right side of the journal page, next to the applicable note. This activity presents readers with a choice of responses and takes them one level deeper in their responding.

As a model, I return to one of my original questions about Jack and Jill:

| Jack and Jill went to fetch a pail of water. | When did this take place? Before people had running water? |
|---|---|

Reflecting aloud, I can see that the event might only matter if the family were poor and if Jack's being out of commission from a "broken crown" meant the family could no longer survive. Who would now get the water? Since Jill "came tumbling after," she most likely is in no shape to take over the household chores. If the family had money, possibly they could hire someone to fill in, even if running water were not available.

| Was the family too poor to afford indoor plumbing? | *With Jack out of commission from a broken head, how will the family survive? Who will fetch the water?* |
|---|---|

My second set of questions, about whether "the crown" was Jack's head or if he were royalty and it was an imperial crown, could make the difference between a realistic story and a metaphoric one, a parable. Maybe Jack went "up the hill" to steal another kingdom's water rights and, in doing so, "fell" and lost his crown or position. This type of response could connect to an international news story and take the reader to an entirely new level of reading.

Let's return to Brittany's journal on *Dangerously Alice* above, in the "Double-Entry Journaling" section of this chapter. At this point, Brittany would place her sticky note on the text that suggested the comparison between the families; note the comparison on the sticky note; and later, on the right side of her journal form, reflect on the significance of this comparison. If the families are indeed alike, how does this affect Brittany's understanding of the plot? Does this mean she can predict that Alice's father will forgive Alice as Brittany's would?

On her three sticky notes in Figure 4.5, Kristin questions, infers, and attempts to interpret a term of art, *break a hundred words*. On the sticky note, Kristin guesses that the term

---

**Figure 4.5**    Sample: Kristin's Sticky-Note Response

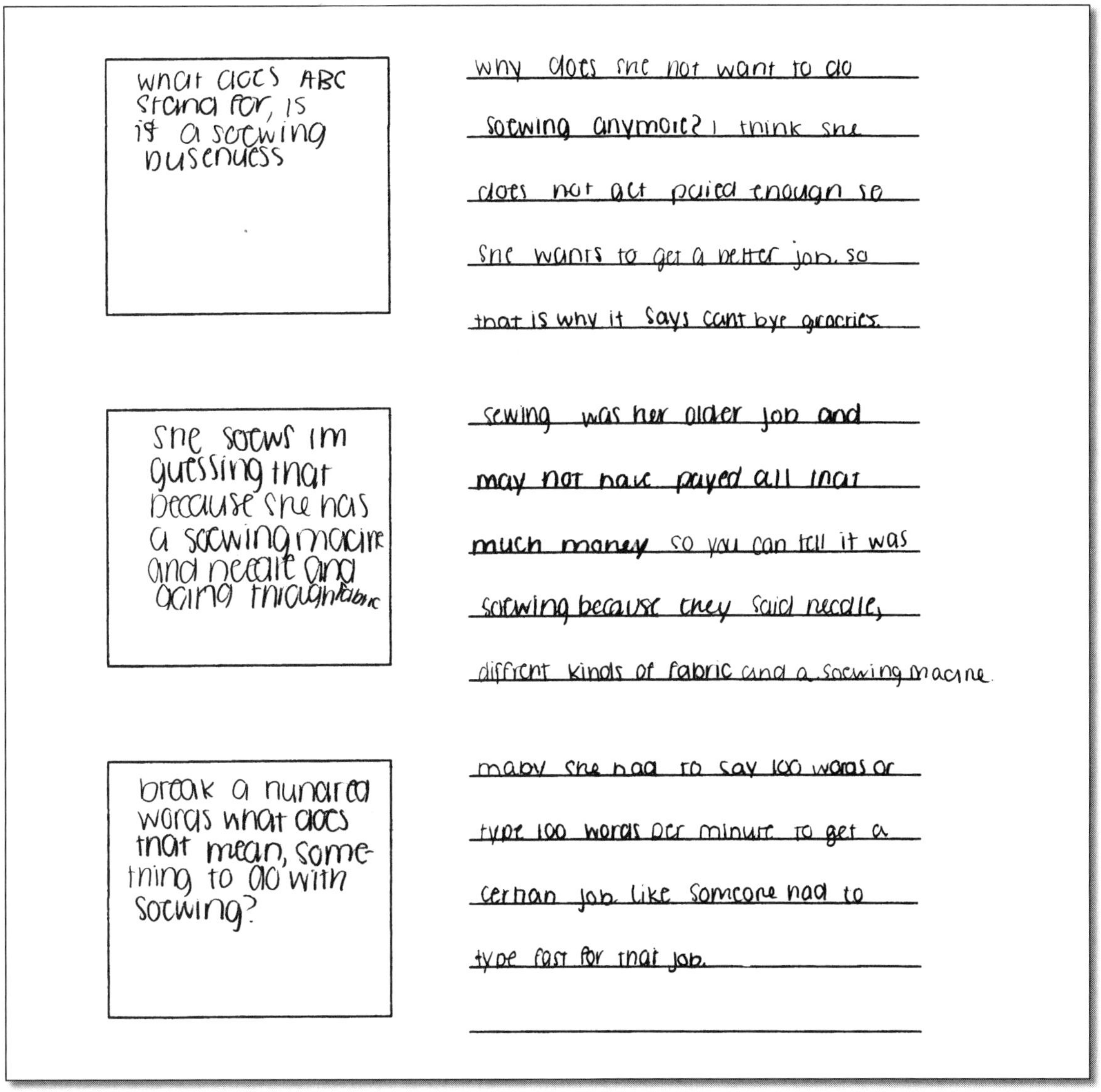

Sticky note 1: "what does ABC stand for, is it a soewing busenuess"

Response 1: "why does she not want to do soewing anymore? I think she does not act paied enough so she wants to get a better job. so that is why it says cant bye groceries."

Sticky note 2: "she soews im guessing that because she has a soewing macine and needle and going throughfabric"

Response 2: "sewing was her older job and may not have payed all that much money so you can tell it was soewing because they said needle, diffrent kinds of fabric and a soewing macine"

Sticky note 3: "break a hundred words what does that mean, some-thing to do with soewing?"

Response 3: "mabv she had to say 100 words or type 100 words per minute to get a certian job. like someone had to type fast for that job."

has something to do with sewing, but when she reflects on her sticky note, she changes that guess to the more accurate interpretation "to type a hundred words per minute."

Sometimes we want students to look for the answers to their questions and then go back to the journal and comment on the answers. Resource B, #12, contains a different type of sticky-note response sheet, a Question-Answer-Response Journal. This triple-column journal sheet includes a column for sticky notes containing questions, a column for the answers found, and a response column for the reader's comment on the answer given (or not given).

## ADAPTATIONS

I differentiate my instruction and my expectations by assigning more or fewer responses for each reading. I might ask my advanced students for two to three entries per day in their double-entry or sticky-note journals and require only one entry for my struggling readers. At first, I require struggling readers to attempt the double entries only once or twice a week, continuing with the format with which they have become comfortable for the remainder of the week. Each week, I increase the requisite double entries. I shift to sticky notes at diverse rates for different classes or students.

As with any five-minute response, I expect more or less writing, depending on the particular student, and I look for more profound interpretations from my proficient readers. I can differentiate the instruction, the requirements, and expectations for each student. What is critical is that each student is moving along a continuum from superficial to reflective reading and from teacher control of response to student choice of response.

# 5

# Poetic Response

We had been studying the Holocaust. I distributed an article about a girl who visited a concentration camp and asked my students to read it for homework. "Write your response in poetry," I instructed.

Groans came from the crowd. "Do we have to?" someone asked. I nodded.

"Does it have to rhyme?" another voice whined.

"Of course not." I explained free-verse poetry. By that time of year, we had studied some poetic devices, mostly rhythm and rhyme, but hadn't read a lot of free verse. I explained that poets used rhyme for different purposes, sometimes to lighten the tone of a poem and sometimes for a more rhythmic quality, but not all poems used rhyme and, in this case, their poems probably wouldn't. "Just capture your feelings," I advised as they left.

The next day they trooped in. As they got out their homework, I asked, "So how was the poetry response?"

A student answered, "The article was so emotional, there really wasn't any other way to respond." Heads nodded in agreement.

Shannon shared her poem:

> Why do you begin to cry?
>
> You say it's time to say "Good-bye."
>
> You should be happy, the sun's so bright,
>
> But the Gestapo points you to the right.
>
> They say to me, "You look strong."
>
> They tell me I'll last pretty long.
>
> "You can lift, and you can heft,"
>
> And so they point me to the left.

I look for you but do not find;

I fear you've left our world behind.

I ask a man—he looks so smart—

What had happened at the part.

He laughs and says, "She went that way?

You won't see her after today.

Never again, not even tomorrow."

He goes and leaves me with my sorrow.

As I look up to the sky,

I know now why you began to cry.

I still use Shannon's poem as a model. I use it as an example of poetic response to the Holocaust, but I also model it to show how a poem *can* rhyme and still portray serious emotion. Students even point out some of the poetic devices, such as the four quatrain stanzas that end with a couplet. I can return to this example later when we discuss sonnets.

Many times I encourage students to use poetic responses, but as with any other reading response, I now *teach* poetic response. I scaffold by choosing a type of poetry, model poetic response in a focus lesson, and have the students practice with a reading assignment. This form of response becomes a part of the toolbox to be used when the reader senses it is appropriate. Some poetic responses work better *during* reading and some *after* reading. The point is to give the readers choices.

## FOUND POETRY

Because it is the easiest, the first type of poetic response I introduce is found poetry. For this type of poetry, the reader uses words and phrases found in the text and forms them into a poem. This is a painless introduction to poetry—What's better than using someone else's words?—but it forces readers to examine the important words and ideas and notice authors' word choices, thereby improving their own. Found poetry also causes students to review the text that they have already read, whether it be a chapter; a section; or the entire article, story, or book.

For my initial demonstration, I use a simple nursery rhyme with which all my students are familiar:

Jack and Jill: The Hill

f
  a
    l
      l
        i
          n
            g
              broken crown!

We then discuss whether the chore, fetching water, was important to include, and we note that different readers may focus on different words. Next I distribute a short news article for practice, and we compare the resulting poems. Students may work in pairs, arguing about the important words or ideas.

For the next week's reading, they are to try this technique one or two times, when they feel it is appropriate. If we are working on a shared novel, I choose a chapter that I feel lends itself to the technique, and it is interesting to compare the resulting poetry. The students ask if they can add their own words to text words, and, of course, they can. Combining their thoughts with the author's is actually a movement towards independence. The day after my students read Chapter 5 of *Waiting for the Rain* by Sheila Gordon, I share my response poem; some of the phrases are from the book, and some are my own.

> Heart like a Balloon,
>
> > excited and intrigued about Reading,
>
> Tengo is drinking up learning
>
> Like the dry ground
>
> > > soaks up Rain.
>
> Getting smart enough to know
>
> > what's going on
>
> > > in the World.
>
> Pent-up Anger,
>
> Knowing that people will never
>
> > > Respect him.
>
> Considered less significant.
>
> The bitter taste will not leave him.
>
> He never had a problem
>
> > until the books
>
> > started coming.
>
> Until he started to
>
> Dream.

That night they attempt a shared poem for the next chapter, and we compare results.

One of my classes was reading Lois Lowry's *The Giver*. After we read about Jonas's assignment at the Ceremony of Twelve and his meeting with the Giver, we took a one-day break to review the first ten chapters and allow stragglers to catch up with the reading. I knew that if I told the students to review the book, those who had already read it would ignore my suggestion, so I taught and then assigned the writing of a found poem. Their topic choices were The Community, Jonas, or The Assignment. My student Mary had not completed many of the class assignments, and I wasn't sure that she was reading the novel. But somehow this assignment spoke to her, and in her poem, I saw that she had, indeed, been reading. I saw as well the creativity—in her use of phrases, ideas, and even fonts—that I had missed so far that year.

THE ASSIGNMENT

<u>Twelve</u>
*No turning back!*

SELECTION
c h a n t i n g
Acceptance
HONOR

Say g°₀dbye.
no longer
*Perfect*

The GIVER
meets

The RECEIVER.
What will
HAPPEN
Next
?

Found poems let students note important details and allow the teacher to see what readers notice and note. The next time I introduced found poetry to a class, I directed them to use the author's words and phrases to make a point of their own. John, reading Chapter 16 of *The Giver,* wrote about what Jonas learned through memories and ended his poem with a lesson that he learned.

Birthday:
1  singled out  1
His Day

Happiness
Room of people
Warm firelight
SN☂WING
Grandparents?

L♥VE?
No pill = LOVE

Lesson:
Enjoy everything that you have.

Cindy, whose class read Salman Rushdie's novel *Haroun and the Sea of Stories*, wrote a found poem, "Haroun's Wish," shown in Figure 5.1.

| Figure 5.1 Sample: Cindy's Haroun Found Poem |

**Haroun's Wish**

The **harder** you wish,

The **better** it works.

I wish.

Eleven minutes passes . . .

*S t r e t c h e d   o u t*—concentrating.

Move the Moon by **willpower?**

Mission accomplished.

The full, hot, noonday sun

Shines down on the Dark Ship.

The world is for *controlling.*

**Khattam-shud!**

After working with found poems, many students feel more prepared to write free verse or even rhymed poetry responses on their own.

## NARRATIVE POETRY

Even though teachers attempt to have readers respond to, rather than retell, the stories they are reading, the ability to summarize is a valuable skill. Many students have trouble with it. I cringe when I think of retellings that went on for pages: "And then . . . , and then . . . , and then. . . ."

The format of the narrative poem encourages conciseness in summarizing either a story or a chapter. The class practices by dividing into pairs, each pair writing the narrative poem summary of a tale with which both students are familiar, as in the following example by Matt and Ryan.

The Three Little Pigs

Once in a town there lived three little pigs,

Who lived in houses made of straw, bricks, and twigs.

They had a problem that was hard to solve,

For the wolf would eat them; it was his resolve.

The pigs would not go down without a fight,

Even if it was one itsy-bitsy bite!

The wolf went to the house of the first pig in town,

"I'll huff and I'll puff and I'll blow your house down."

The pig stated, "Not by the hair of my chinny-chin-chin,"

*And hoped the wolf wouldn't have him for his din-din.*

The poor little pig had only a house of straw,

And then his house had a really big fall!

He ran away and had a sigh of relief,

When he saw a house of twigs and one little leaf.

He asked the pig inside if he could stay,

And told the story of how the wolf blew his house away.

The second pig agreed, and they saw the wolf comin';

They had to make a plan or do a little somethin'.

The wolf came to the second pig in town,

"I'll huff and I'll puff and I'll blow your house down."

The pigs both stated, "Not by the hair on our chinny-chin-chins,"

*And hoped the wolf wouldn't have them for his din-din.*

Since the house was not strong enough,

It blew into piles of little bits of stuff.

The pigs ran away and saw a house of bricks,

And told the pig inside about the wolf and the house of sticks.

The wolf came again, but to the third pig in town,

"I'll huff and I'll puff and I'll blow your house down."

The three pigs stated, "Not by the hair on our chinny-chin-chins,"

*And hoped the wolf wouldn't have them for his din-din.*

**The pigs all worked together to make a plan,**

While his blowing sounded like a trumpet in a band.

He tried another way and jumped down the chimney,

But he didn't know that a waiting pot was steamy.

> The wolf was burnt and ran away.
>
> The three pigs were happy and smiled the rest of the day.
>
> The wolf was gone; he was no more.
>
> ***While the pigs went to get house supplies at the store.***

Matt and Ryan's poem based on "The Three Little Pigs" illustrates that, even though the poem is a faithful retelling of the story, we can also see where the readers made *inferences* and *predictions* and that they got the **point**.

In independent reading, some students like to try one stanza per chapter to write the epic of their book or one stanza per night as the reading response for that night. In this way, the weaker writers can also write a narrative poem, one night at a time.

The narrative poem of a novel illustrates how the chapters and characters fit together. While Amanda was reading *Monster* by Walter Dean Myers, she wrote a narrative poem about the protagonist, Steve Harmon, who is in jail, awaiting his trial.

Monster

> Steven Harmon was convicted of a harmful crime;
> Now Steven, you see, has to do a lot of time.
>
> His young mind floats away every night,
> He thinks of things that happened—so harsh a sight.
>
> Steven used to dream of a good life with wife and kids too,
> But he threw it away, choosing the wrong thing to do.
>
> "Guilty" or "not guilty" is what the jury is thinking,
> While poor Steven is sitting there, his life just sinking.
>
> Mothers, fathers, baby siblings too—
> Just remember, they're all affected by what you do.
>
> He made a fool of himself, something he will never forget.
> Always think before you do something that you will regret.
>
> Now he sits in his cell thinking how his life could be,
> If he weren't involved in the crime they see.
>
> His friends betrayed him; they lied and stole.
> They also took Steven's heart away, whole.
>
> He lost his honesty and reliable name—
> And that which he thought would bring him fame.

Amanda's poem proves that the narrative poetry response can reach beyond simple retelling to an analysis of character motivation and reader evaluation.

Narrative poetry particularly lends itself to collaboration as an after-reading text reformulation (see Chapter 9). For example, book club members can write a narrative poem of their novel to share with the class. One class wrote a collaborative narrative poem of their shared novel, *The Giver,* as a review of the plot; each student wrote one stanza per chapter.

Some students go a step farther when writing narrative poetry. I had already taught limericks, and a few weeks later, I gave students the opportunity to retell *Haroun and the Sea of Stories* in a narrative poem as one of many response choices. When Jen handed in her assignment, I noticed, to my surprise, that not only were the main points of each of the 12 chapters summarized in a stanza but each stanza was a limerick! While using this form was not something I would ever require—we don't want the form to overtake the purpose—it allowed her to use her creativity, and she most likely had to review the text deeply to find details that fit her format. I particularly noticed that she did not just choose events that rhymed but made a conscious effort to have the rhyme and rhythm fit the important details, an incorporation of the higher thinking skills of application, analysis, and synthesis. The poem begins with Chapter 1:

> There's a storyteller named Rashid,
>
> His wife's return is what he needs,
>
> Haroun is his son,
>
> Their only one,
>
> And now Rashid needs his stories indeed.

And it ends this way:

> The Sea of Stories is saved;
>
> Haroun is considered brave.
>
> His mom came back;
>
> Rashid's stories no longer lack.
>
> A happy ending is what the Walrus gave.

## POEMS IN TWO VOICES

A portion of shared reading for my language arts classes consists of multicultural literature. But when modern American students study literature of another time and place, I often note a detachment—recognition, even compassion for, the plight of *them*, not *us*. The students in our school district are not significantly diverse; therefore, multicultural experiences through literature are essential. However, to be meaningful, a relationship must exist between the readers and the characters—real or fictional.

When the classes read *The Diary of Anne Frank,* even though students were acting out the drama, I noticed a lack of empathy for the young girl who lived and died during Hitler's regime. Could it be that my students—50 years and 5,000 miles distant from Anne's life—did not feel any connection to her? My dilemma was how to help my readers make that connection, and I turned to two-voice poetry. I first introduced "Honeybees" from Paul Fleischman's *Joyful Noise: Poems for Two Voices*. This poem, like the others in the collection, compares the lives of insects. Similarities are read simultaneously, in two voices, while differences are read individually. I partnered with a student volunteer, and we dramatically presented the poem that compares the lives of the queen bee and a worker. The queen bee explains why, to her, "Being a bee is a joy," while at the same time the worker complains, "Being a bee is a pain."

In this poem, Fleischman contrasts lives that, to humans, might appear to be more alike than dissimilar. My job was to teach the students to compare, or *connect*, two lives that might appear to be more divergent than similar. I clarified the concept of poetry for two voices and shared my experience comparing myself to Esmeralda Santiago, author and main character of the memoir *When I Was Puerto Rican*. As an example, I read a poem I had written called "Teenagers." Then I explained the assignment: each student was to write a two-voice poem entitled "Anne and Me."

On the day the assignment was due, I found that everyone had been able to complete the task. The students selected partners, practiced reading their poems aloud, and then presented the poetry to the class. The readings were incredible, powerful beyond my expectations. These modern, suburban, relatively secure American teens had found commonalities, beyond age, with Anne Frank.

Mary wrote this:

---

**Me & Anne**

| | |
|---|---|
| *A teenage girl,* | *A teenage girl,* |
| **I live in** | **I live in** |
| Freedom. | |
| | Hiding. |
| **I am** | **I am** |
| Roman Catholic. | |
| | Jewish. |
| **I am optimistic.** | **I am optimistic.** |
| | Out-going. |
| Easy-going. | |
| **I love attention!** | **I love attention!** |
| *I am* | *I am* |
| Obedient. | |
| | A Rebel. |
| But **I am going to think** | And **I am going to think** |
| **what I want to think.** | **what I want to think.** |
| | European |
| European-American | |
| Summer Camp | |
| | Concentration Camp |
| **Alive today** | **Alive today** |
| For a long time | |
| | But not for long |
| Reading **a diary** | Writing **a diary** |

**about Anne Frank.**

---

These associations were not limited to the girls of the class; the boys, to their surprise in some cases, also discovered resemblances between Anne and themselves.

After the presentations, I asked students to reflect and comment on the experience. Mary wrote,

> Despite differences in time or appearance, people can be similar to each other. We may be different in many ways, but we are similar too. We all have emotions and personalities and, despite color and creed, we all connect in different ways. Sometimes prejudice gets in the way of that.

Debbie commented, "Writing and reading this poem aloud really gave me the feeling that she [Anne Frank] was a living, breathing person and not just a character in a book." Bridget made an interesting observation: "Writing this [poem] made me look deeper into, not only Anne's personality, but my own." Martin credited the power of the comparison to "the form . . . the two voices." In these reflections, students were analyzing and evaluating their poetic responses, taking response to a metacognitive level. The class undeniably had a compelling experience through this writing format.

I decided to revisit the two-voice poetry format when one class read *Waiting for the Rain* by Sheila Gordon, a historical fiction novel that depicts the lives of two boys, one white and the other black, growing up in South Africa under apartheid. I asked my students to compare Tengo and Frikkie. Doing so would allow, or even force, them to look at both sides of the issues. They would have to explore the conflicting points of view of two boys who were raised under this system, a system of separateness— of *us* and *them*. I invited my students to examine thoroughly the characters, their backgrounds, their experiences, their educations, and their hopes and dreams to ascertain how it might be possible for the two boys and, with the fall of apartheid, the two races to work together. Again, students rose to the occasion, as shown in Amanda's poem:

| *Frikkie:* | *Tengo:* |
|---|---|
| **I am growing up in South Africa . . .** | **I am growing up in South Africa . . .** |
| **My family** owns **a farm.** | **My family** works on **a farm.** |
| I live in a house; | |
| | A hut; |
| I am the "kleinbaas." | |
| | I, just a servant. |
| **I get an education** | **I get an education** |
| **because I** have **to.** | **because I** want **to.** |
| I want to work. | |
| | I want to learn. |
| **I wish I could** stay on the farm. | **I wish I could** get away. |
| | I fear the army. |

| *Frikkie:* | *Tengo:* |
|---|---|
| I am in the army.<br>I fight for my country. | |
| | I fight for my freedom. |
| **I wish things would** not change.<br>**Apartheid**<br>**Protesters**<br>**Violence** | **I wish things would** soon change.<br>**Apartheid**<br>**Protesters**<br>**Violence** |
| My friend Tengo is Black. | |
| | My friend Frikkie is White. |
| **He says that I am not being fair.**<br>There is nothing I can do. | **He says that I am not being fair.** |
| | I am doing what I can, but |
| **One person cannot change things alone.** | **One person cannot change things alone.** |
| I am fighting for my country.<br>I am just obeying the law. | |
| | The law is wrong. |
| **This land really belongs to my people.**<br>They cannot have it. | **This land really belongs to my people.** |
| | But we will share it. |
| My people will grow up to be<br>Doctors and lawyers. | |
| | And my people will be<br>Servants and laborers. |
| **Our people were here first.**<br>I am defending my country. | **Our people were here first.** |
| | I am defending my people. |
| **We must agree and work together**<br>**If we are to live equally.** | **We must agree and work together**<br>**If we are to live equally.** |

Throughout the remainder of the year, some students continued to employ this format—when they found it appropriate. Calvin was an amazing basketball player but a reluctant reader and writer. I introduced him to the books of Walter Dean Myers, and in *Hoops* he found a connection with a character and, therefore, a new connection to reading. Calvin's poem tells his story:

---

**Me & Lonnie**

*We are two kids trying to make it to the NBA.*

I am about to graduate from middle
school

                    I am about to graduate from high
                    school

*And play basketball for*

My high school.

                    My college.

*I'm kind of scared, not knowing if*

I'm going to play varsity or JV.

                    I'm going to start on a good team.

*Right now,*

I'm getting ready for my eighth-grade
dance.

                    I'm getting ready for my Senior Prom.

*I'm just a boy, taking my steps into manhood.*

Today I take the PSSA test.

                    Today I take my SATs.

**In two months I'll be off** to the        **In two months I'll be off** for college.
high school.

*Who knows what the future might bring?*

---

That same year, Lou discovered gang, or street-life, novels and formed text-to-text comparisons as he noted the similarities between two characters, Rufus of *Durango Street* and Ponyboy from *The Outsiders*. What was remarkable were not the similarities in the characters but the differences Lou noted and the reasons why they were similar despite the differences. One tends to stereotype gang members, but we can see that Lou went beyond stereotypes in relating to these characters. When I use this poem as a model, I point out that the poet didn't just include random facts about each character—each fact that he uses makes a point. Maybe if their neighborhoods weren't "trash," Ponyboy and Rufus wouldn't feel the need to be in gangs. It doesn't matter what color they are or who their enemies are; it matters more where they live and, possibly, that their fathers are gone. It doesn't even matter that both are somewhat involved in gang leadership, Ponyboy through his brother; they both "hate being gang members," hate being in a society where membership is necessary for something to do and even for survival. While Ponyboy has his brother to "look out for him," Rufus takes care of his sister—a difference; nevertheless, they both "would die for [their] families." The last line points out a feeling that *all* adolescents have—that they are uniquely different, even though they want to blend in.

---

**Gang Life**

PONYBOY (*The Outsiders*)                    RUFUS (*Durango Street*)
White

                                                                    Black

**Gang Members**

I'm a Greaser.

                                                                    I'm a Moor.

**Our neighborhoods are trash.**

Our enemy is the Socs.

                                                                    Our enemy is the Gassers.

**We are poor hoodlums.**

                                                                    I live with my mom;

I have no parents.

**Our dads are gone.**

My brother looks out for me.                 I look out for my sister.

**We would die for our families.**

My oldest brother leads our gang.

                                                                    I lead our gang.

**We hate being gang members,**
**But we need to do something.**

My gang is my family,

                                                                    I want to leave my gang,

**But we're not like other hoods.**

---

Poetry in two voices lets readers demonstrate and evaluate the text-to-self, text-to-text, and text-to-world connections they make by comparing themselves to a character, two characters from the same text, and two characters from different texts.

# I AM . . . POETRY

Another effective poetic response form, either during or after reading, is the "I Am" poem. The typical format for this poetry is shown here, but the verbs can be modified either by the teacher or by the reader-responders to fit their characters and texts.

| I am [name of character] | I pretend . . . | I understand . . . |
|---|---|---|
| I wonder . . . | I feel . . . | I say . . . |
| I hear . . . | I touch . . . | I dream . . . |
| I see . . . | I worry . . . | I try . . . |
| I want . . . | I cry . . . | I hope . . . |
| I am . . . | I am . . . | I am [name of character repeated] |

I have used this strategy with shared reading, book clubs, and individual reading. When the entire class reads the same novel, I divide the class into the same number of groups as the number of characters in the book. Each group collaboratively writes an "I Am" poem for its character and then decides how to present it. I introduce techniques of oral interpretation and choral reading, such as echoing, repetition, varying speed and volume; individual, duet, unison, cumulative, or alternating reading; and the use of emphasis and pauses for effect. Students can even choreograph the movements of group members. For book club presentations, the club members can individually write an "I Am" poem for a different major character, and the group can collaboratively decide how to present the poems, such as how they might portray the relationships between and among characters. This also serves to place an equal focus on secondary characters and their goals and motivations. Students can dress up as the characters and, in this way, present their book to the class.

In the same way, during our study of *The Diary of Anne Frank* and the Holocaust, my students wrote "I Am" poems based on their individual readings when I handed out identification cards of Holocaust victims provided by the U.S. Holocaust Memorial Museum. Each student adopted a victim and read the brief biography, and some conducted additional research. Then each wrote and presented a poem.

Tyler read the biography of Bernard Greenspan, a young man who witnessed the atrocities of the Holocaust and survived to do something about it.

Bernard, born in Rozwadow, Poland, on March 6, 1911, was one of five children born to a Jewish family in the southern Polish town of Rozwadow. His father, a World War I veteran incapacitated as a result of the war, supported his family on his military pension. In the early 1930s Bernard completed high school and worked on the family farm.

1933–39: In 1934 I was recruited into the Polish army and stationed in Lvov, where I ran a canteen. After three years there I returned to my family's farm outside Rozwadow to work. On September 24,

1939, the town was captured by the Germans. Some in Rozwadow were happy to see the Germans; soon afterwards some townspeople began looting Jewish stores, while the occupying forces looked on. The Germans even made films of the robberies.

1940–44: In 1942 I used false papers to get to the town of Stryj [Stry] where, posing as a gentile Pole, I got a job in a sawmill. While at work one day I heard gunfire. I watched trucks carry Jews to a nearby clearing bordered by bushes; German machine gun nests were concealed in the brush. Jews were run off the trucks and onto bridges spanning a huge ditch. Then guns ripped, catching the people in the cross fire. The shooting went on all day. After work, I saw the clearing's freshly turned earth move. Were some still alive?

Bernard joined the Polish partisans in late 1943. After the war he remained in Poland until emigrating to Israel in 1957. He moved to the United States in 1960.

As Bernard, Tyler reflected as follows:

I am . . . Bernard Greenspan, an average Jewish soldier.

I wonder . . . What will my family, my brothers, do? Run, fight, or hide?

I hear . . . gunshots tearing through innocent flesh, another hole in the world.

I see . . . glass shattered like crystals, fire, and blood.

I want . . . to live, to survive, the end of war.

I am . . . amongst the fire, yet not consumed.

I pretend . . . that I'm a Gentile, a peaceful neutral.

I feel . . . pain, hatred, and longing for my family.

I touch . . . the blade of the mill and feel the suffering of my people.

I worry . . . for all who cannot escape, cannot flee, cannot move.

I cry . . . I am not a Jew, but a Gentile, and save my own skin.

I am . . . on an island amidst a lake of fire.

I don't understand . . . why this is happening.

I dream . . . of death, pain, and the end of the war.

I try . . . with the Resistance to show we have hope.

I hope . . . to get my life back—my friends, family, and farm.

I say . . . Why must we die? Why the sick, old, and the young?

I am Bernard Greenspan.

Samantha poignantly responded to the biographical sketch of Max Rosenblat, a young child who died during the Holocaust. His identification card shared the facts of his life:

Max's parents, Taube and Itzik, first met as children in 1925. Taube was the daughter of a tailor who hired apprentices in his shop, and Itzik was one such apprentice. The Jewish youngsters fell in love and dreamed of getting married even though Taube's family frowned upon the match.

1933–39: In 1938 Taube and Itzik married. The couple lived in an apartment on 49 Zeromskiego Street in Radom, where Itzik opened a women's tailor shop. Max was born in July 1939. He had curly hair and blue eyes like his father. Two months after he was born, Germany invaded Poland. The Germans occupied Radom and evicted all the Jews from Zeromskiego Street. The Rosenblats had to leave everything, even Max's baby carriage.

1940–42: Radom's Jewish Council assigned the Rosenblats to a shack, which was enclosed in a Jewish ghetto in April 1941. Max slept in a homemade bed of straw. He had no toys and little food. In August 1942, when Max was 3, the Germans began rounding up and deporting all the Jews in Radom's two ghettos who could not work for them. Max's father tried to hide his family in his shop, but they were caught in a roundup and Max and his mother were taken away. They were marched to the railroad and herded into a boxcar.

In August 1942 Max and his mother were deported to the Treblinka extermination camp, where they were gassed upon arrival. Max was 3 years old.

Sam's poem reveals her inferences about and insights into what Max may have been thinking and feeling:

I am Max Rosenblat.

I wonder where I'm going on this crowded train.

I hear sobbing, strange voices, and people quietly praying.

I see my Mommy's wide, frightened, brown eyes.

I want to be in her arms forever.

I am a scared three-year-old boy.

I pretend I am safe.

I feel so cold, my teeth are chattering.

I wish we could get off this train and go home.

I want to play and run in the sun!

I try to hold back my tears and be a brave boy.

I am so thankful to be with Mommy.

I don't understand what's happening.

I whisper, "Mama, where's Papa?" and she starts to cry.

I dream of food, a warm bed, and toys.

I hope to see Papa again soon.

I was just a little boy who died before I had a chance to really live.

Nicole read the biography of Dora Rivkina, and after the experience of writing and performing her poem and listening to others, Nicole reflected, "As I wrote, I put myself in Dora's shoes and sort of felt and heard and saw her living through this rough time period." She continued,

> The experience of listening to the other poems [of classmates] made me realize how lucky I am for being alive. . . . It was almost scary to think of kids our age being killed because they didn't look German or weren't a specific religion.

The poetry put her into the text she was reading and made it come alive.

## THE ADVANTAGES OF POETRY

At this point, readers are able to choose the appropriate poetic format for their responses or take off in their own, individual directions. Students sometimes research additional poetry forms or remember forms taught in poetry units of former years, and some try haiku or limerick responses. These poetry formats address the reading strategies I teach, such as noticing important details (found poems), visualizing (concrete poems, such as the "Jack and Jill" response), summarizing (narrative poems), connecting (two-voice poetry), and inferring ("I Am" poems). For questioning, I sometimes use Shel Silverstein's poem "What If?" Students can than muse on the direction of their novels' plots and characters' lives and decisions.

Supplementary poetic forms can be used to focus on literary devices. For example, acrostic poems can force students to delve into characters' personalities, decisions, and relationships, although not typically at the level of an "I Am" poem. Haikus can be paired with settings to illustrate the mood established by the setting, noting the author's descriptive words and images.

While poetry should be taught as only one type of response, to give readers choice and to be used when and if appropriate throughout the rest of the year, teaching it has many advantages. Teaching poetry responses also teaches poetic devices and, therefore, serves as a "twofer"—two lessons in one. Students who become skilled at these formats and devices can then apply them to poetry writing in general. Another advantage is that students become comfortable with writing poetry and have a repertoire that they can then expand, building on to what has become prior knowledge.

Additionally, students who would never imagine writing poetry become poets. For the tentative, the text provides a scaffold for writing since it gives a basis for content. I have found that, as students become comfortable with writing poetry, they write poetry not only as reader response but also for diverse assignments, such as personal memoirs.

It is always beneficial to exhibit student work—both as models and to celebrate students' skills and creativity. Poems are effective displays because other students can easily pass by a bulletin board and read them and poetry can be attractively formatted and presented. I find that students are interested in each other's poetic responses, especially to shared reading texts or when they are responses to the same assignment, such as the "I Am" poems.

Over the years, as response has become a daily occurrence for my students and as readers try out an ever-increasing variety of responses, I find the reactions, in many cases, expanding and becoming even more profound than those of previous years. This year, Helen Ann responded to Dara Horn's "Walking with Living Feet" from the October/November 1993 issue of *Merlyn's Pen,* the article about the Holocaust mentioned at the beginning of this chapter.

We Will Not Forget

Majdonek,
Still intact.
At any moment,
It could brutally murder
Once again.

Standing there in that murky
Chamber,
I hear them shriek
Their cries of torture,
The sting
Of never-ending pain.

Blue streaks stain
The cold, clammy room,
Matching the scratches
Still tearing at the walls,
Left by those who couldn't escape.

They cry out,
But no one will hear;
No one will care.

The feeling of ghostly
Fingers pull at my skin.
They still want to be saved
Though they are gone.

My lungs tighten,
Short breaths
Just
Barely
Escaping.

Yet not far
From this prison of death,
Are homes—

People's homes
Where there are parties
And holidays.

No one noticed this hell.

Hats,
Toothbrushes,
Hair
Fill these dark barracks.

Five,
Five are filled with
Shoes—
850,000 pairs:

The shoe of a mother,
A father,
A son,
A friend.
Every shoe different,
But all the same.

I can see my shoe.
And your shoe.
And my mother's shoe.

I entered the same way
They did.
But fate led them
A different way
Out.

A picture is worth a thousand words,
But not a thousand feelings.

Being in their presence,
I know
I can never forget.

# 6

# Interactive Response

## NOTE PASSING

This is my dream. I'm standing in front of the classroom. My students are reading a shared text individually, or I am reading a text aloud. Out of the corner of my eye, I see it—the little folded, white paper making its way up the aisle. I stare in disbelief. *Note passing in my classroom?* I pounce and apprehensively confiscate the note. I open it, ready to chastise the students at their inattentiveness to their lesson and the misguided focus on their social lives. Not one to embarrass students publicly with their secrets, I read the note to myself: *Isn't this story awesome? I never knew that a kid could be a detective. Do you think*

**Figure 6.1** Note-Passing Cartoon

*Source:* Matt Roessing, 2009.

*that he will figure it out? I think it's the neighbor.* I stare in delighted disbelief. She is writing about our story! I wake up.

This scenario is not as ludicrous as it may appear. Middle school students love to communicate with each other, and they love to write notes to each other. Admittedly, the subject is usually the past weekend or a cute boy or girl, but they rationalize that if they are writing, they are not interrupting the class, and they also are not risking being overheard by the nosy student in front of them. The same is true of any note passing, even academic. "Silent talk" is less disruptive than a roomful of small groups chatting, especially to those students who have fragile attention skills or limited focus. And writing notes is writing; any writing gives writers more practice at refining their thoughts than speaking. When writing responses, readers find out what they know and want to say and what others know and want to say.

I use a note-passing activity with the texts that are more challenging, that may require more thinking or interpretation, or with which I especially want *all* students in the class to interact actively. We were reading Daniel Keyes's short story "Flowers for Algernon" as a shared text. I usually read the beginning and the end aloud because there is no punctuation and because I like to stop and discuss along the way. At one point in the story, I stopped and asked the students to analyze the protagonist, Charlie Gordon's, idea of friendship. I then asked them to pass these "notes" to their seat partners, who responded to this response directly on their partner's note. Even though definitions of *friendship* are, to some extent, personal, my students are used to working with their partners and do not have trouble sharing information that is not exceptionally private. They were very interested to see what another reader thought—about Charlie and about their ideas about Charlie. Figure 6.2 is one example of a passed note on Charlie and friendship.

When we reached the middle of the story where Charlie's IQ is normal or above normal and, therefore, his writing is comprehensible, I directed the students to read independently. I then asked them to write down their responses to that section—their inferences, questions, predictions, etc. Prior to class, I placed the desks in groups of three. After we read and responded for a few minutes, I built on the previous note-passing experience, informing the students that they would be passing their responses to another student in their group, who would respond in writing to their responses. After another few minutes of response, they would then pass their notes to the third student, who would respond to anything written on the paper. Since these were not particularly personal responses, I was not concerned how students were grouped. Because of the nature of the text, students did not go off in extremely divergent directions, but their responses were somewhat varied. Moreover, even though many had similar predictions, in numerous cases they based these predictions on different evidence. As these comments show, they found the exercise interesting and helpful:

> "I liked the note pass because we can actually interact with each other about class work without talking."—Jamie
>
> "I was shocked to see that people agree with me."—Dawn
>
> "I was surprised that everyone agreed with my thoughts about Charlie."—Amanda
>
> "I was glad to see that Dominique and Karim agreed with me completely. This means to me that we were all on the same page."—John

While many of the proficient readers are more interested to find that their interpretations branch off in divergent directions, the less confident students are relieved to find that their analyses are similar to those of others. To them, agreement means they are on the right track; it means that their answers meet with peer approval. I find that many

**Figure 6.2** Sample: Anthony and Andrew's "Flowers for Algernon" Note Pass

Drew

March 10 to April 3rd

Charlie's notion of friendship is very different than mine of anyone else I know. He thinks that anyone that laughs when he is around and likes to hang around him is his friend. His two best friends laugh at him, not with him like he thinks. It's kind of a sad thing really. On top of laughing at him, they ditched him and left him out in the cold after a drinking party. I think the cop was more of a friend for taking him home than Frank and Joe have ever been. From being sick, having a headache and from hurting all over, I think Joe and Frank were terrible friends.

Anthony

I agree completely. This kind of what I wrote in my response. It's not right for two guys to take advantage of person like that. The cop really saved Charlie from danger because, who knows where Charlie would have gone, had he not been taken home by the policeman.

times, students are reluctant to share their opinions with the class because they are certain that no one will agree with them and that they will be perceived as not making sense.

Some students combined the two sentiments—their responses were validated while some contradictory thinking was expressed. Samantha pointed out "they mostly agreed with everything I wrote when I wrote it down," but also that "when I read theirs [the notes that the other group members initially started], they had different comments [about the text]."

Nick wrote,

I'm surprised that Shawn agreed with most of my response. However, he did not agree that Charlie will become a neurosurgeon. I thought he [Charlie] would want to use the experience as a learning experience and figure out new ways to do the surgery.

Rather than becoming discouraged, Nick is learning to defend and support his thinking. I credit this to the fact that someone "agreed with most of his response" and that Nick had a chance to read, reflect on, and answer Shawn's reply (and that Shawn's disagreement was given in the privacy of the note). This gave Nick, a very shy young man, a chance to consider if he wanted to share his prediction with the class.

To differentiate instruction, teachers can manipulate the groups initially so that students who respond at certain cognitive levels are placed together in groups until they become familiar with the exercise. The groups can then be made more diverse so that struggling readers are able to view the responses of stronger readers, which will help them to grow as responders. This combination not only lets less confident students see the responses of others before writing their own, but it also gives them three chances to respond to something that the group reads. And after the first writing, they will have one, two, or three models. On the other hand, heterogeneous grouping encourages stronger readers to become more tolerant of the responses of struggling students as they read their responses and see how those students formulated them. Sometimes skillful readers will communicate their scorn, verbally or nonverbally, for weaker, faulty, or even inappropriate responses when given orally in class.

I find that note passing becomes especially beneficial when students are responding to poetry. Students seem to think that there are "right" and "wrong" interpretations of poetry, as if the poet had whispered into the teacher's ear. And many teachers perpetuate this myth. Students need to learn to respond to and even interpret poetry in their own way, but they do appreciate their fellow readers' help. Note passing takes away the threat of submitting oral comments to an audience of 25 to 30. It narrows the audience and allows readers to see how responses and interpretations can diverge in different directions, all of which are "right." "The Road Not Taken" can literally be applied to poetic response. The first time I implemented note passing with poetry, I could almost hear sighs of relief as students read each other's responses to the poem and the responses to their own notes. "The other responses helped me to understand the poem," and "I found that we all thought differently but everyone had reasons for their thinking," were the two most common appraisals of the note pass.

In one class, my students were tackling a complex poem, "An Anti-Semitic Demonstration" by Gail Newman. In one of the triads, one student focused on the description of the street, another began with the inference that the poet's mother was Jewish because of the numbers on her arm, and a third thought the poem might depict the Nazi invasion of Poland. As the readers worked out their thoughts through the note pass, they each finished with a refined version of their observations and interpretations, some retaining many of their ideas with a few adjustments or additions, and some revising their analyses based on group members' responses. This time, when the notes returned to their originators, I directed the students to read all the responses and write one final response. I instructed them not to respond back to the others or write about whether they agreed with the other responses but to write a new response to the poem based on their note "discussion." I invited them to observe if they now noticed different aspects of the text or looked at the poem in a different way. All final responses contained more elaboration than the original responses, even though the students had been given less time to write.

Note passes give students the rehearsal and confidence to participate in class discussions of texts and guide them to deeper comprehension of texts. Through the notes, students expand their own ideas and contrast them with others—ideas that they have had the chance to consider and reconsider in the light of other ideas. If an idea doesn't make sense, the group members point it out in the relative privacy of the note. This "off-the-record" activity allows students to become secure enough to share ideas orally in class later, knowing that their peers also do not hold all the ideas, and the entire class profits through added class discussion. For struggling readers, writing responses in their own groups also gives them ideas, either their own or those of others, to share in whole-class discussions.

I asked the students what *they* saw as the advantages of the note pass or, as we called it that particular day, "silent discussions."

> "There are no interjections or interruptions by other students. I can finish sharing my idea, even if I have to stop and think."
>
> "My questions got answered."
>
> "There is time to get my response out and make changes before anyone reacts to it. If I forget what I am going to say, I have time to recapture the thought without other students staring at me."
>
> "I can remember what everyone else 'said' by rereading what they wrote."
>
> "There is no 'off-topic' conversation."

Two additional benefits are that everyone takes part in a discussion, multiple times, and that note passing provides me with a record of my students' thinking.

## FAMILY LETTERS

Once a year, I ask my students to write a letter to a parent, guardian, or other family member and to request a response. This letter is to be written about their reading so far that year: *what* they read—books, genres, topics—and *how* they read. They are also to write specifically about the books they are currently reading. I find the winter holiday break an opportune time for this activity. I want my students to continue reading during the vacation but do not want to encumber them with daily journal responses, as many have other obligations. I do ask them to continue to log in their reading dates, times, and pages, and I suggest that they read for 25 minutes for a majority of the vacation days. I point out that reading aloud to younger siblings or to older relatives is reading. Instead of the daily journal responses, I assign a family reading letter.

The reading letter serves multiple purposes. Students write about what they are currently reading, and in this way, their letter serves as vacation response. Drafting the letter causes readers to examine and to reflect on the reading they have done thus far that academic year (and perhaps even plan their future readings). They are writing about books and about reading, and most importantly, they are communicating these thoughts to their families—in most cases, their parents. During adolescence, any communication is rare and appreciated by parents.

They are to ask the family member, the addressee of this communication, to respond in writing. Not only do students rarely discuss their academic curriculum and their reading habits with family members, it is also uncommon for parents to discuss their reading practices with their children. I have found that parents respond to this assignment in a variety of ways. Some react simply to their children's reading; some write about their own reading patterns and strategies and share what they are currently reading; and some reflect on books they read when they were adolescents, at times revealing that they read some of the same books. No parents have declined to answer their adolescent's letters, although some responses have been "interviews" transcribed by the student. In a few cases, the parents did not speak English, and their child wrote down their responses, one adding her own comments in the margins.

Alexis wrote to her mother about the Shadow Children series by Margaret Peterson Haddix. "This week I am reading *Among the Betrayed.*" She continued by writing a plot outline with some annotations and then critiqued the books' author:

> Margaret Peterson Haddix is a really talented author; the plots of her books are filled with surprises that I couldn't have predicted. Although I wish that she had developed the characters of Percy and Matthias. Alia seemed to be the only one of the three that was fully developed. Maybe they could have played a bigger role if Nina knew more about them. It seemed that they were just really smart and knew how to escape from the "prison." I definitely will read all the books in this series. Hopefully Margaret Peterson Haddix is writing more than just the five that are already out.

Her mother responded:

> Dear Alexis,
>
> I am thrilled that you are enjoying the series of books by Margaret Peterson Haddix. I understand how a book can capture you and reel you in its intrigue. These are the types of books I enjoy most. M. P. Haddix is a very talented author. I was thrilled with the first in this series, Among the Hidden. I'm glad you took my advice and gave this book a try. Recommendations are a great way to learn about new books and new authors. I hope you pass this recommendation along to a few friends. The next best thing to reading a great book is discussing it. Good luck with your future reading.

Alexis's mother reiterated sentiments I had been expressing all year, but they were more powerful coming from her.

Nicole and her mother also wrote about recommending books to each other. Nicole related having read a variety of genres that year. Her mother responded, "I am happy this [reading] is a passion that we share," and agreed how important it is to read "books from different genres." She continued about a book, *The Glass Castle*, that she had read on Nicole's recommendation. "It was a great book. It is fun discussing books with you. I have some to share with you by my favorite author, which is Jodi Picoult."

Tom wrote about *The Inquisition War* by Ian Watson and asked his father if he ever had an object take him back to a childhood memory as one of the characters did. His father replied with comments about Tom's reading and his book and then shifted into the memory of the property where he grew up. Their letters shared text-to-life connections.

Lauren's mother ended her letter with encouragement for future reading: "I hope that you continue reading for the rest of your life. Your choices of books have been great. Keep reading, keep learning and growing, but most of all keep enjoying your reading." Teachers can lecture all they want, but nothing is more valuable than support from home.

Not only did Samantha's mother endorse the importance of reading—"Reading is so important; hopefully you will make time to read the rest of your life. I wish I made more time for it myself."—but she also pointed out the enjoyment of reading together—"It was nice to read with you during Christmas Break. Even though I read *Summer of My German Soldier* to help you, I really did enjoy it." Her letter also contemplated an added advantage of reading her daughter's books: "Maybe I should read the books in your Clique series. If anything, it should help me better understand you and your crazy friends, kind of like research!"

My students are as interested in these replies as I am. When asked about the letter-writing experience, many students echoed John's sentiments: "I was very happy to see that my parents were interested in my reading." Dawn added, "It [my parents' letter] showed me that the schoolwork I do means something to them." Tyler responded to her mother's account of her own past reading habits: "It was cool because I got to see some genres and books my mom read when she was my age." She was seeing her mother as an adolescent and as one who read, validating herself as a reader. Likewise for Chrissy: "Now I know from reading her [my mother's] letter how much in common we have with books and the kinds we like."

Many times, parents become their children's reading buddies through this activity. Ed said that his "mom thought that I read some cool books and some that she even might like." I have had students not return books when they finished reading them because "my mom is reading it now." I try to buy two copies of books; initially I did this for student reading buddies, but now I can suggest parent reading buddies.

## LETTERS TO FRIENDS

I suggest that my students, besides writing to family members, write some responses as letters to friends when they have finished a book. These letters can serve as their evaluation response, because they will be writing about their book—the plot, the characters, the writing—and whether and why they would recommend it. To be authentic, they should write to a student who would actually be interested in this type of book. In this way, the letter differs from a typical book review. It becomes a discussion, a personal suggestion. As an interactive activity, readers can request that the addressee write back, either about the recipient's interest in the book based on this recommendation or about books the recipient thinks the writer may be interested in reading, based on this letter.

Sometimes readers don't wait until they finish reading a book to recommend it:

> Dear my friend Colleen,
>
> I strongly suggest you read the book I am reading. I like how the narrator really tells you what is happening. I am halfway into this book, and I feel as if I was there, seeing every moment of Steve's horrible life. I feel really sad while reading this book because it is about a boy who is in jail. *Monster* is one of the best books I have ever read because you feel like you know the characters. If you enjoy reading realistic fiction, this is truly the one for you.
>
> Your friend, Amanda

This letter was written early in the year before we discussed evaluation, but Colleen can see that, even partway through the book, her friend Amanda recommends *Monster* by Walter Dean Myers but with a restriction—Colleen needs to like to read realistic fiction to enjoy this book. Amanda shared the basic premise of the plot ("It is about a boy who is in jail.") and that the story evokes emotional reaction. Colleen also now knows that Amanda reads a lot of books and that, so far, this is "one of the best books [she has] ever read."

## CO-READING LETTERS

Students are always invited to read books together. I usually have two copies of novels, and pair reading can serve as a precursor to book clubs. When one student is reading the same book as another student, I encourage the readers to write responses to each other. I use as an example my responses to fellow language arts teacher Mrs. B (see Chapter 3) and share her responses to me. The students can see that at times we are responding to the text and at other times we are responding to each other. I suggest that teachers first try this activity with another colleague for the experience, as well as for the authentic models it provides. Unlike book clubs, students do not have to keep to the same reading schedule, as long as they don't give away important plot elements. I have suggested that students mark their responses by chapter, as I did, so that their partners do not read that part of the letter before they have read those chapters themselves. Other students wrote letters to coreaders until they read much farther ahead and then abandoned the letters to return to individual reading journal entries.

## TALKING ABOUT TEXTS

"Talk about what you read last night [*or* just now]." I see a group animatedly chatting and gesturing. I gleefully slip over to that side of the room. Words like "football game," "Saturday night," and "new boyfriend" waft through the air. I sigh and look around for another group. There's one—the members staring at one another, each praying someone *else* will say something. A third group thumbs through their books, feigning fascination with the text (or their desks).

**Photo 6.1**   Brianne and Hollie talk about a text

Many teachers begin response with talk: "Turn and talk," "Pair share," "Say something." I do just the opposite. I find that at the beginning of the year, adolescents do not know what to talk, say, or share unless it is about their social life or friends. Many are only comfortable talking to their friends. Talking strategies may work well with elementary readers who are less self-conscious about their ideas or in front of other children, but early adolescent talk is either off-task or falters and expires. There are two reasons for this: the students have not yet formed a reading community where they trust others with their thoughts about reading, and they do not know what to say about the reading.

Readers need to be trained in response and practice it in writing. At first, they serve as their own audiences as they reflect on their reading; then I am their audience as they submit their journals and look for my comments. Not until after those experiences are they ready to be each other's audiences, first in pairs, then triads, and then larger groups leading into book club discussion groups (see Chapter 7). At the beginning, it also helps to ask readers to write down their responses before they share them orally. When a student's partner replies, the response discussion becomes interactive. Teachers can number the individual students in pairs as #1 or #2 and specify when each is to talk, training them to take turns and not to dominate the discussion or interrupt the speaker.

At the beginning of the year, I seat students in pairs with seats six rows across in a modified semicircle or modified *V* so that students can view the board but also face some of their classmates and feel a part of a community. Each row contains four to five desks, depending on the class total. I design the space this way so that they become comfortable with a partner, so that no one feels left out in a mad scramble to form pairs, and to save time. Having six desks across the room, they can also easily divide into triads. I find it advantageous for pairs to sit side by side; if desks face each other, talk needs to be louder, and readers cannot merely point to something in their books. Of course, when there are groups of four, and sometimes three, students need to cluster their desks. As the year progresses, the groups can expand, but I usually limit size to four or five unless a specific project requires additional people or the class has an absentee problem.

It is necessary to be specific about oral responses. Teachers often tell adolescents to "turn and talk" and are surprised when they do just that. While it might be obvious to some that they are to talk about the reading done, either their own or responding to a read-aloud, some adolescents accept this as an invitation for personal talk. We practice with read-alouds, incorporating our daily focus lesson. I might say, "Turn to your *partner* and *talk* about the character traits that Sally shows," "In *pairs, share* a connection you made to the story, a time when you were disappointed in someone," or, "*Say something* to your partner about the author's use of description, for example your favorite image." Because they were directed to do so and because they know to whom to talk and specifically what to say, students do not feel strange talking about the text. As the year and lessons progress, we talk about our shared readings—short stories, poetry, articles, and our shared novel—and classmates become more at ease with their community and with oral response. At this point, directions can become more general (e.g., "Make a prediction."). Ultimately, readers can begin to talk about their independent readings with each other.

Teachers need to *teach* oral response and train students to develop each other's ideas into a conversation. "Did you have the same prediction as your partner(s)? If so, why? If not, why not? It is okay to disagree with something that is said in your group as long as you can support your statement with the text." We need to let students know that literary disagreements are based on different interpretations of text; they are not personal, and differing opinions can each be "right." We can also teach struggling students to piggyback onto the comments of another, even saying, "I agree because . . ." I might say, "Share with your partner(s) if you, or your character, had the same experience as theirs."

Strategies and skills of group talk are further developed through literature circles and book clubs. Once the scaffolding has been put in place, the structure becomes secure enough to remove as students gain control of their literary talk. By the end of the year, students may be talking more than writing. Through their journaling experiences, they learn to form their thoughts more quickly and coherently, and they accumulate multiple strategies for response and become familiar with using literary "lingo." Even more vitally, readers now have an audience; they are members of a literate community that writes and talks about literature—just like in the real world.

## COLLABORATIVE RESPONSE

When we studied the Holocaust as background to our reading of the play *The Diary of Anne Frank,* my readers were giving similar responses to articles and text providing the historical background:

> "This is terrible."
>
> "I cannot believe this happened."
>
> "How did this happen?"

My students were reacting as the 21st-century, relatively safe and secure American youth they were. I decided to try another tact and had them read an article about the invasion and capitulation of Holland from differing points of view. The students numbered off 1–4, and I gave the following assignment:

1. Read the article "Nazi Terror Moves to Holland."

2. In free-verse poetry, respond to any applicable part of the article as

   (a) a Dutch Gentile citizen.

   (b) a Dutch Jew.

   (c) a Nazi.

   (d) a member of Anne Frank's family.

My goal was to move my students to deeper reading and responding. I chose free-verse poetry so that they could use actual words and phrases from the article (*what* to say) and so that they could think about the power of their line breaks (*how* to say it).

First they read and drafted their verses. Then they reflected on the advantages and disadvantages of reading from a particular viewpoint. Grace wrote in her Journal,

> Knowing that I would have to respond to the article entitled "Nazi Terror Moves to Holland" from a Nazi's point of view, I paid close attention to what the Nazis were doing. I focused on how they treated the Dutch people and how they acted.

> I tried to imagine how a Nazi, filled with hate, would view the world and the people in it. However, because I was focusing on the Nazi's point of view, I think it detracted from my reading. I wasn't paying attention to how the innocent people acted when it didn't affect my story. I was thinking a lot about what I was going to put into my poem, instead of focusing on all of the information.

This comment led to a discussion about the effects of bias on reading.

Next the students formed groups, each group containing each of the four points of view, and they read their verses to each other. Afterwards, they reflected on the experience. Katy wrote, "I got a different aspect on it [the information] when I listened to the other points of view in our group. They showed all four sides, which helped me to understand the entire story." Grace, who had written that when she read to write as a Nazi, she only focused on certain events and information, echoed many of the students' feelings by responding that after listening to all four poems, she saw the overall picture created by the article.

This is a different style of "jigsaw" reading. In a typical jigsaw, each group member reads a different portion of an article and, without reflection, reports back to the group so that no one needs to read the entire article. This technique is only as effective as the different readers. In the point-of-view reading, all group members read the entire article, chapter, or section of book, and the students' divergent reflections served to pull it together. It becomes a collaborative way of responding and, therefore, learning.

In one group, Grace responded as one of the Nazi troops who invaded Holland, while Jenna responded as a Dutch citizen:

---

Grace's Poem

I am a Nazi
On my way to Holland.
We invaded their country,
Weak and foolish.
They thought they could stop us,
But nobody can.

We bombed their great city Rotterdam.
The Dutch did not surrender
To us, the great and powerful Nazis.
If they think they can stop us now,
They better think again.
At least a few of them
have some sense,
which they showed by joining our fight.

They cannot escape.
They can try to run or hide,
But there is nowhere for them to go.
One day the Nazis will rule the world
With Hitler, the ruler of it all.

How dare the Dutch try to fight us
Even the filthy children tried
To hurt us with their prince's flower
That we ripped from their lapels.
Yes, the razorblades cut our fingers.

They should enjoy their small victory
While they have the chance.

---

Jenna's Poem

Holland was a place of freedom.

No Jews would be harmed here;

We were a neutral place.

Hitler promised to stay away.

That was one of his empty promises.

We were prepared for Nazi invasion,

Even for Case Yellow,

The operation to invade Holland.

We tried to protect the Jews.

They were accepted as the Dutch citizens they were.

In five days we were defeated

And forced to surrender.

The air was so thick with smoke.

It was 3 days of night following the bombings.

The shrieking still haunts me; I was 13 years old.

Though we surrendered,

We had not given up.

There was a will to resist Nazis among all Dutch people.

Those who sympathized with them were spit upon and ignored.

Even the children fought back.

Nazis had immediately sent Polish Jews to ghettos and camps.

They were harassed and beaten;

Not in Holland though.

Anti-Jew campaigns started slowly.

Nazis knew mistreating Dutch Jews would only antagonize the rest of us.

The Jews relaxed, thinking they were home free.

They were sadly mistaken.

It started just two months later.

The laws were passed one by one.

In a little over a year, Jews became prisoners of the Nazis.

Life was no good for us either.

They started shipping out our goods and foods,

Even our gas and electricity.

Hundred of us died of starvation daily–

Jews and non-Jews alike.

We Dutch still put up a fight.

The consequences of our action were soon learned.

Those who defended the Jews,

Were treated like Jews.

This included: beating, torture, life in prison, forced labor, and death.

In spite of this, Christians would show sympathy by wearing yellow stars.

In February 1941, the first anti-Jew riot broke out in Amsterdam.

Jews and Dutch friends fought back.

Irate Nazis took to the streets with tanks

And ran down hundred of people.

During these riots if one of their own were injured,

The Jews were punished.

400 were sent to concentration camps when one Nazi policeman was shot.

Dutch dockworkers were outraged, and went on strike.

*(Continued)*

(Continued)

Nazis answered with martial law; anyone who disobeyed them was shot.

Though there was no way to stop the Nazis,

We tried until the very end.

Catholics would continue to aid Jews.

The penalty was severe.

20,000 Catholics were sent to concentration camps.

I remember on July 1942, the Nazis began deporting Holland's Jews.

This was the day we were all dreading.

Every week thousands were called to report,

Supposedly for "resettlement for labor in the east."

We knew better than that.

There was nothing anyone could do still.

Nazi search squads would round up Jewish families.

With clubs and machine guns, the captives were ushered to the streets.

I remember clearly the heartbreaking looks on women's faces,

As they begged strangers to take their children.

Most of them took in the Jewish children.

Thankfully many of them survived the war with the Dutch families.

As I saw them load into the cattle carts,

Like animals on the way to the slaughter house,

My heart wretched, I knew their fate, as did so many of us.

They were headed to one of two camps.

Both were in Poland, and both were equally disturbing.

I've heard about their journey just to get there.

Their cart had no seat, heat, or bathrooms.

Most didn't survive the several-day trips.

I knew that I would be lucky to see any of my neighbors' faces again.

The war would not be over for three years.

And I know that because of us we may have helped.

We held the Nazis off as long as we could.

We fought 'til the very end.

Lindsay responded to the article as a Dutch Jew:

### Lindsay's Poem

I lie awake in the dawn time,

It is May 10, 1940,

The Dutch troops line up,

For the Nazis are coming.

To take Holland for themselves.

Hitler wants to rule the world.

He makes all these silly laws,

For me and the other Dutch Jews.

Like the Jews in Germany,

We had registered "for our protection."

But now he uses that against us,

The people who own businesses and walk around.

Because now we must wear our star,

The star we used to honor,

Yellow, four inch wide star on our shoulders and front window.

We now cannot blend in.

We now are becoming hungry,

As we only eat sugar beets and flower bulbs,

Trying everything to make them better,

But nothing ever works.

Our Dutch neighbors

Helped as much as possible,

But the Nazis kept getting tougher,

And there was no way to stop 'em.

Then that tragic month came,

Of July 1942,

The Nazis bring the trains

That are to take us to the East.

The day before they came to Amsterdam

I had gotten a call-up notice.

The only thing I could do

Was to go into hiding.

Because I had heard the stories

That were told person-to-person

About the railroad cattle cars

And where they took you.

I had heard some heartbreaking things

That I really wish to not speak of,

How people die on those cars

Before they can even get to the gas chambers.

So, I finally went into hiding,

Like a lot of Jewish people did,

Because in Holland times were rough,

So I had to protect myself.

In her analysis, April, who was assigned to write as a Nazi, wrote that she "did not wish to write as a Nazi." In fact, she "thought it would be easier to write from one of the Franks's point of view." However, she then reflected, "I think it was best for me not to have [written as a Frank family member] because I learned a lot about the Nazis that I probably would not have known." April's evaluation of the group collaborative reading-response experience makes a noteworthy point: "When we shared our readings, I noticed that there was only an enemy. Whether it was the Jews, the Nazis, there was always an enemy."

This collaborative response strategy works well with any shared reading. In a fiction text, readers can respond to a poem or a section or chapter of a novel from the point of view of different characters; many times, in this way, students notice things they ordinarily would have missed. Collaborative response is also adaptable to reading in any content area. It lends itself particularly well to social studies text. However, I can see reading health articles, possibly about disease, from the point of view of a patient, a doctor, and a researcher. In science classes, environmental articles especially lend themselves to differing points of view. Readers could then debate, based on information from the same article.

Interactive response aids students of all abilities since it gives them an opportunity to respond with others. With such a range of possibilities, each one offering support from other readers, minimal adaptation becomes necessary.

# 7

# Literature Circles and Book Clubs

## *Discussion Response*

The students sit in circles, four or five in each circle. Novels, reading journals, and writing implements lie on their desks. An observer of any group would most likely see one adolescent talking while the others listen, one or possibly two indicating that they want to add or challenge something, a few thumbing through their novels or glancing at the notes in their reading journals, and some adding to those notes. This class looks very different from a few weeks before, when students sat in semicircular rows, desks pushed together in pairs. The class has moved from whole-class discussions to literature circles and book clubs.

Although the terms can be used interchangeably, I differentiate between *literature circle* and *book club* experiences. I refer to literature circles when the class is reading a shared text but students meet in small discussion groups. I employ literature circles as training, or rehearsal, for book clubs. Because we are all reading the same novel, I can control the reading schedule and move students from group to group if necessary or desired for divergent discussion experiences.

## LITERATURE CIRCLES AS TRAINING

I introduce literature circles three-fourths of the way through our shared novel, after students have learned and practiced double-entry journaling and sticky notes, note passing, and literary talk and they have reviewed and applied multiple reading strategies.

The most significant aspect of literature circles is discussion, which, like any response technique, needs to be taught. I begin with a shared poem or short story. In the demonstration, I first show readers how to maintain a response dialogue by assembling a few other teachers or even some of my students to read a poem or watch a television show and then stage a "fishbowl" discussion in front of the class. The spectators write down and discuss in small groups what they noticed about our conversation. One year, I discovered that three students had watched the same episode of *House* as I; quite coincidentally, the episode dealt with some of the same tolerance issues we were discussing in class. It was an ideal demonstration because it was very natural. When we came back together as a class, spectators had noticed that "everyone contributed to the discussion," "people took turns," "it sounded like conversation," and, most importantly, "everyone brought up different issues and supported their points with examples from the show." This last may have occurred because the participants knew that the audience had not viewed the show, but it served as a powerful model. I was gratified by the other comments as well, because I wanted my students to see that discussion should be a natural response.

When I demonstrate with other teachers, we read a poem because it is short enough for the class to refer quickly to copies distributed to them and because responses to poetry diverge more frequently than those to other writings. While the discussion participants are encouraged to jot down notes, we do not practice the discussion in advance, nor do I direct what to say. I may suggest topics to observe—poetic devices, imagery, and vocabulary or tone—because the colleagues participating are not necessarily language arts teachers. In fact, it is more effective when students observe content area teachers chatting about a poem and hashing out "meaning." Thus readers realize the benefits of group discussion; it takes note passing (Chapter 6) a step farther.

As the next step, students are placed into groups, either randomly or by design, to discuss the current chapters of their shared novel. I teach them how to develop discussion points rather than discussion questions. The difference is that with discussion questions, students feel they have done their jobs if they come up with good questions and may not even contemplate any answers or, conversely, may come up with specific answers and answer their questions themselves. When they come up with discussion points, however, the students will also participate in the discussion. Since we are all reading the same chapters, I can demonstrate how to develop a discussion point or, with struggling readers, can provide discussion points to guide them, since we are focusing on interactive *response* at this time. An added advantage is that students can move from group to group and groups can compare their conversations about the same points or compare the points brought up in their meetings.

## BOOK CLUBS

The final step, when students put these guided practices into independent application, is the movement to book clubs. In book clubs, small groups of students are reading texts selected by members of the group. The selection process determines the composition of the groups. I display and book-talk the choices, and students write down three preferences. With three options, I can manipulate the groups if necessary. Even though young adolescents are very social, they usually are relieved to find themselves with students they like but are not their best friends so that the peer pressures of social conversation don't outweigh their interest in the book or their wish to perform well in the book club. I have had students observe that their groups were effective "because I was *not* with my friends."

Before students browse the books, I ask them to write a preliminary reading response. If the book clubs are based around a theme, such as the effects of intolerance on human rights, I ask them to freewrite about the theme. If the clubs are based on a topic, such as the Holocaust, I might ask them to make a K-W-L chart listing what they already know; what they want to find out; and, as they read, what they learn about the topic. If the clubs are genre based, perhaps around folktales or memoir, I might ask students to freewrite in that genre or to respond about the genre itself.

As they look through the books to determine three choices, readers are to think about *why* they might want to read a book. On a Preference Form, they write each of their choices, accompanied by a "Why I Chose This Book" response (Chapter 2). This way, I know that they are scrutinizing the book and that their decisions are based on criteria other than the fact that their friends are considering the same book. Their responses let me assess their commitment to each book and whether they actually determined that the book was on their reading and interest levels.

Once the book clubs are formed, the members plan their group reading and discussion schedules. They plan to meet every other day, alternating with writing workshop, and I give them a projected finish date. The class follows a specific agenda on book club days (see Resource B, #13). We commence with a short whole-class focus lesson demonstrating a discussion procedure or teaching or reviewing a reading strategy, literary element, or genre structure on which readers will focus in their conversation and next reading. During the following book club meeting time, readers discuss the text read, and the class ends with reading time during which individuals can read ahead independently or club members can read aloud to each other. Since the individual clubs cooperatively plan their own reading schedules, they can determine when they want to read more or less—on weekdays or over weekends; starting slowly and then moving more quickly as they become familiar with the plot and the characters or reading more at the beginning when there might be less to discuss. Many clubs simply divide the book pages or chapters by the number of meetings. The clubs also collaboratively make other logistical decisions, such as how to handle members who are not current with their reading or responding because, as with all reading, readers are expected to continue their Reading Journals.

## BOOK CLUB RESPONSE

Like many teachers, the first time I implemented book clubs, I took Harvey Daniels (2002) literally and assigned roles for book club meetings. I copied the role sheets on colored paper and had students switch roles each club meeting day. Each group had its Discussion Leader, Visualizer, Connector, Vocabulary Evaluator or Word Wizard, Question Asker, etc. Immediately, I discerned three problems. First, the students simply went around the group, reading from their papers or showing their pictures, in sequence. When they completed the circle, they were "done." Second, a major problem for the groups was absenteeism—no Discussion Leader, no discussion. And the principal problem for the readers themselves was that each role focused on one particular reading strategy, whereas we want students to employ multiple or appropriate strategies, especially in this phase. For example, visualizers envisioned the text but were not accessing other reading strategies or, at best, were unaware of doing so, making them somewhat ineffective in any discussions other than those about descriptions.

After that first year, I significantly modified the response process for book clubs. Each club member became responsible for partially fulfilling all roles. My book club response form is a double-entry journal like the one students were using with their shared novel but adjusted for book club reading (see Resource B, #14). Members are *each* responsible for a short summary of the chapters read so that they can refer back to the events of the chapters that are the focus of the meeting. They also can see what events each found important to write down; this helps the weaker students to focus on important details. In the left-hand column on the reverse side of the form, they are to note (1) a discussion point; (2) a choice of an interesting quote, a visualization, or something else they noticed in the text; (3) a new or interesting vocabulary word; and (4) a question, inference, or prediction. In the right-hand column, readers write their responses to whatever they recorded in the left column.

I explain the homework assignments, pointing out that these journals will be the basis of their individual homework grades for the novel and will provide support for their group discussion. Either verbally or on a handout, I explain as follows:

> As you read, you are to continue your Reading Journal with a special book club form to use in your group discussions and then to hand in. For each meeting it will contain the following:
>
> *I. On the front:*
>
>> a) On the top half: A summary of the text read to which you can refer; you can simply list the main events that occurred in the chapters. New characters and settings should be highlighted in two different colors.
>>
>> b) You can use the bottom half for any notes taken during the whole-class focus lesson or in discussion group or for any background information researched or learned (for more advanced texts).
>
> *II. On the back is the double-entry journaling form.*
>
>> The left column, "From the BOOK," will contain
>>
>>> 1. a discussion point to bring up;
>>> 2. a good quote, an example of figurative language, or a character or setting description to share;
>>> 3. an interesting or new word, the sentence in which it appeared, and its definition; and
>>> 4. a question, an inference, or a prediction.
>>
>> The right column, "From Your BRAIN," will contain a response to or reflection on what you wrote in the left column, as before.

I show them some examples:

| From the BOOK | From Your BRAIN |
|---|---|
| 3. (p. 1) **cosmopolitan** *adj*: worldly, sophisticated, of the whole world | I guess that people who live in cities are cosmopolitan; I was surprised that this word could refer to persons *or* products. |
| **ant** INEXPERIENCED | |

| *From the BOOK* | *From Your BRAIN* |
|---|---|
| 2. (p. 1) When asked how they survive the winters, he said, "They wear coats." | I think he's being sarcastic. Of course, they survive the winter. He must mean that they dress appropriately for the climate. |

At this point, students may be more comfortable using sticky notes as they read (see Chapter 4). They can then transfer those notes to the left column and respond to them in the right column. Figures 7.1 and 7.2 show one student's book club journal response.

By continuing with double-entry journals, readers are not just remarking, they are reflecting, and the book club members have multiple concepts to discuss, no matter how many group members are absent. Even if group members note the same word or make similar predictions, each will have something different to say about the response. In fact, that is just what makes a conversation. And I find they rarely "finish" their discussions since there is such a wealth and variety of topics. They may start out the first day going "around the circle," but as soon as students find something in common, a conversation ensues:

> "I put down that same word, but I wrote that I remembered that it was in *The Giver.*"
>
> "Oh, right. I forgot about that. Was it the same form? I think that we had the noun *transgression.* Remember, Mrs. Roessing made the drawing of the speeding car and the speed limit sign."
>
> "My word can be a noun or a verb also."

I find that, once the barrier is broken, club discussions rarely regress.

**Figure 7.1** Ceire's Book Club Response—Page 1

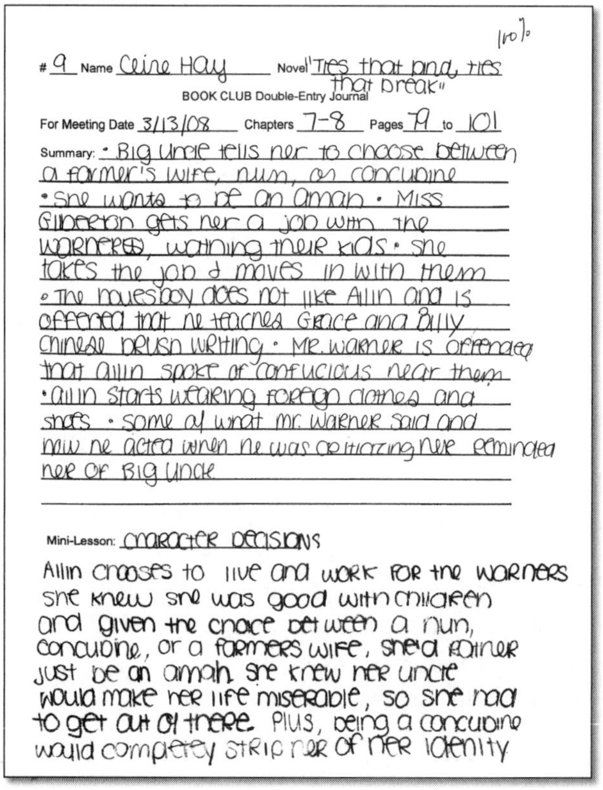

100%

\# 9 Name Ceire Hay Novel "Ties that bind, ties that break"

BOOK CLUB Double-Entry Journal

For Meeting Date 3/13/08 Chapters 7-8 Pages 79 to 101

Summary: • Big Uncle tells her to choose between a farmer's wife, nun, or concubine • She wants to be an amah • Miss Gilberton gets her a job with the Warners, watching their kids • She takes the job & moves in with them • The housboy does not like Ailin and is offended that he teaches Grace and Billy Chinese brush writing • Mr. Warner is offended that Ailin spoke of Confucious near them • Ailin starts wearing foreign clothes and shoes • some of what Mr. Warner said and how he acted when he was critizing here reminded her of Big Uncle

Mini-Lesson: Character Decisions

Ailin chooses to live and work for the Warners she knew she was good with children and given the choice between a nun, concubine, or a farmers wife, she'd rather just be an amah. She knew her uncle would make her life miserable, so she had to get out of there. Plus, being a concubine would completely strip her of her idenity

**Figure 7.2** Ceire's Book Club Response—Page 2

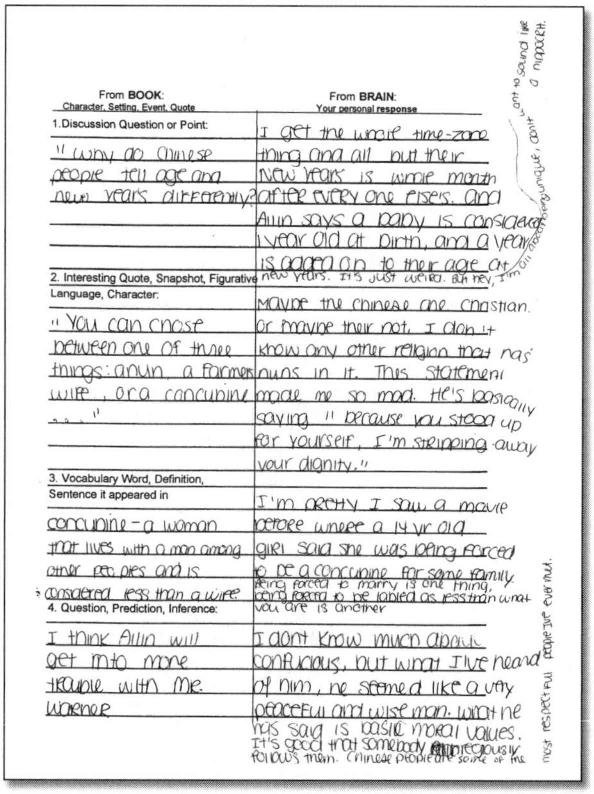

| From BOOK: Character, Setting, Event, Quote | From BRAIN: Your personal response |
|---|---|
| 1. Discussion Question or Point: "Why do Chinese people tell age and new years differently?" | I get the whole time-zone thing and all but their New Years is whole month after every one else's. And Ailin says a baby is considered 1 year old at birth, and a year is added on to their age at new years. It's just weird. But hey, I'm all about being unique, don't want to sound like a hippocrit. |
| 2. Interesting Quote, Snapshot, Figurative Language, Character: "You can chose between one of three things: a nun, a farmers wife, or a concubine ..." | Maybe the Chinese are Christian. Or maybe their not. I don't know any other religion that has nuns in it. This statement made me so mad. He's basically saying "because you stood up for yourself, I'm stripping away your dignity." |
| 3. Vocabulary Word, Definition, Sentence it appeared in: concubine - a woman that lives with a man among other peoples and is considered less than a wife. | I'm pretty I saw a movie before where a 14 yr old girl said she was being forced to be a concubine for some family. Being forced to marry is one thing, being forced to be labled as less than what you are is another |
| 4. Question, Prediction, Inference: I think Ailin will get into more trouble with Mr. Warner | I dont know much about Confucious, but what I've heard of him, he seemed like a very peaceful and wise man. What he has said is basic moral values. It's good that somebody religously follows them. Chinese people are some of the most respectfull people I've ever met. |

Written responses assist the shy members and the forgetful students in contributing to the conversation. The double-entry journals have additional advantages. The journal sheets prompt those who have read ahead and are not sure exactly what text the meeting is to cover; response is more valuable when written at the actual time of reading. Another benefit is that journaling provides a record for revisiting a past discussion point. For assessment purposes, the journal pages make it obvious who has read the assignments and give the teacher something objective to evaluate. I visit the clubs as an observer, but the journal pages allow me to keep current with the discussions and to monitor individual comprehension. If students are absent for any book club meetings, they remain responsible for maintaining and handing in their response journals.

As valuable as the response journals can be to contributing to the club discussion, there is no requirement to cover those responses during the meetings. Conversation during meetings can be so rich that participants may find themselves not even referring to their sheets. The cognitive act of having responded while reading can carry over into the meeting, and one simple statement can engender a multifaceted conversation. Also, through discussion, readers' ideas may change from their initial reactions in their journals, rendering what they wrote obsolete. However, for those whose memories need a nudge, the journals are a resource and support.

I have observed a direct correlation between the use of a response sheet with a variety of reflections and a lively, extended discussion. I feel that if students can engage in and sustain an on-topic discussion when I am not in the classroom to supervise and encourage them, the system is working. Heather, my substitute for a day, took notes on book club discussions in a heterogeneous class comprised of some reluctant readers:

*Durango Street*—All four students were equal in the conversation. Talking about gangs brought in other knowledge (documentary on TV) to help explain what the characters are going through. They made predictions of what might happen

**Photo 7.1**   A book club meeting: Da'Sha, Andrew, and Alayna

next. Talking about a character who had "disappeared." All four talked about what they liked/disliked about the section of reading.

*Down a Dark Hall*—Members took turns responding to questions. They were analyzing characters—talking about their motivations and making predictions of what they might do. Pretty even with contributing to the discussion.

*Hoops*—They were trying to figure out something that was unclear—what "sentences" are. They finally came to a consensus that they were jail sentences. Nick seemed to lead the group, but they all asked questions (good ones!). They took turns giving opinions/insights.

All the groups stayed on-task the entire 20 minutes!

The double-entry journals fit as a natural element of the group meeting and, as a component of the yearlong Reading Journal, add to each student's individual reading record. As part of their preliminary training for book clubs and for the gradual release of control, the class members try at least one of these book club double-entry journals at the end of the shared novel in a literature circle and then in a whole-class discussion. Since the class is reading the same novel, I can prepare an example based on the previous night's reading or even the previous day's discussion. When they share their journals the next day, I can also share a journal page since I am reading the same novel; students can then compare mine to theirs, which sometimes sparks its own discussion.

Students can also circulate to other book clubs to share their new or interesting vocabulary words or figurative language or to compare author descriptions or even protagonists or settings. Students who create more advanced—more issue- or theme-based—discussion questions can also observe how their questions can apply to different novels. This works particularly well, and should be built into the meeting schedule, if book clubs are planned around a common topic or theme.

One additional type of written response I expect from my students is a reflection on and evaluation of their meetings. After the formal meeting ends, I ask members to fill out, individually and independently, a Book Club Reflection Form (see Figure 7.3) on which they analyze and evaluate the effectiveness of their meetings. After each club concludes its meeting, one representative picks up Reflection Forms for the other members. (I prefer that they distribute them *after* the meetings so that they are not filling them out *during* the meetings.) Members reflect individually and submit the forms on their way out of class (as an exit pass). These forms should take less than five minutes to complete. Teachers can revise the forms periodically to reflect different procedures being taught as the book clubs progress. They can be modified to provide not only for self-assessment but for assessments of the other club members' contributions to the meeting. Figure 7.4 shows one student's completed Book Club Reflection Form.

When the book clubs finish reading and discussing their books, each club is required to collaborate on a book presentation of their choice. The dual goals of these presentations are post-reading reflection and sharing books with the rest of the class, thereby providing other students with ideas for books they may want to read independently. Detailed information and examples of text reformulations as after-reading activities are discussed in Chapter 9: Post-Reading Response.

**Figure 7.3** Sample: Book Club Reflection Form

Book-Club Reflection (Write neatly and be specific.)

Today we discussed . . .

_____

From our discussion I learned . . .

_____

An interesting point made was . . .

_____

A question I still have about the book/What I want to find out now is . . .

_____

I felt that the meeting (circle) was/was not effective—successful—because . . . (refer to procedural lessons)

_____

| What I did well today + | What I need to work on – | What I tried to improve = |
|---|---|---|
| ___ listening and responding | ___ sharing information | ___ new ideas/insights |
| ___ turn taking | ___ including all members (eye contact) | |

**Figure 7.4** Sample: Jessica's Book Club Reflection

Jess

BOOK CLUB REFLECTION (Use this as a model each day – Write neatly)

Today we discussed: The first 50 pages of Habibi and how she felt Moving from St.Louis to Palestine.

From our discussion I learned: We learned that the war against Jerusalam and Palestine is still going on today.

An interesting point made/ An answer to a question I had was: I thought an interesting point was when we all asked how we would feel if we were Liyanna.

I felt that the meeting went well because we all had something to say and relate to. We stayed on topic.

| What I did well today + | What I need to work on — | What I tried out = : |
|---|---|---|
| + listening and responding | + sharing information | + new ideas and insights |
| _ turn-taking | + including all group members (eye contact) | + staying on topic |

A question I still have about the novel — or — What I want to find out now is I want to know what's going to happen next! I'm begging to really like this book.

## ADAPTATIONS

Book clubs, by their nature, lend themselves to differentiated instruction, for students choose books at their own reading levels. The books offered should deal with interests appropriate to adolescent readers but be at diverse reading levels. I have purchased four or five copies of books in different genres, topics, and reading levels but have also found that I can borrow from other teachers' libraries or class sets of shared novels, not only from my grade level but also other grades, providing a range to my readers. However, I have noticed that some readers will feel, if the topic or plot interests them, that they can choose books a bit above their reading levels; they know that they have the support of their club, especially after their first book club experience. Selecting three book choices also gives teachers leeway to manipulate the groups to best suit their readers' skills and learning.

Another way to provide differentiated instruction is through the response sheets. Rather than using the sample form, teachers can revise or even abridge response forms. Teachers can require that in the left column, students list a question, a detail they think might become important, a connection, and a visualization, thereby reviewing the reading strategies. Another form might ask readers to note on the left a character, a setting, or other literary element and comment on it on the right. For struggling readers, the teacher can provide general discussion questions (e.g., What character trait made the protagonist act the way she did?), either typed on the response form or given to students, so that they can choose one for the next meeting. The strength of the response form is that it can be customized to the needs of individual clubs or students, as can the book club experience. Thus, this work prepares them for the next stage—the individual reading workshop.

# 8

# Individual Reading

## *Relinquishing Control and Giving Choice*

A student from another class walks into my classroom. She looks around quizzically. Four students are lounging in "comfy chairs" (the camp chairs in the back of the classroom), two students perch on floor pillows, one is stretched out on the carpeted floor itself, two others are sitting at a table, and the rest are sitting in a variety of positions at their desks. All are reading, but they are reading different books, their reading journals within reach. Except for two students who are reading the same novel ("partner books") and discussing a passage, only the sound of turning pages and occasional chuckles, or tears, breaks the silence. "Cool!" she says and hands me some papers.

It *is* cool that adolescents are so comfortable reading and responding. When I read, I don't sit at a small desk; I get comfortable, and so should they, as much as classroom limitations allow. I keep clipboards and bowls of sticky notes handy so those sitting away from their desks are able to write about their reading. We have finished our focus lesson for the day, and students are now reading and responding for at least a half hour. This is my time to confer with students whose reading responses have indicated some comprehension problems or students whom I feel I can take deeper into their novels. I also walk around and surreptitiously note page numbers to compare with Daily Logs. I confer for about half the period, and I read for the other half. I feel that it is important for students to observe adults reading. This also provides some time to catch up with recently published or student-recommended adolescent literature that I can then book talk, recommend, or use in future lessons.

By the beginning of March, my students have had a variety of literary experiences. We have read shared short texts—short stories, poetry, and magazine and news articles—during class as components of focus lessons on reading strategies and literary elements, while reading independent, self-selected texts as homework. We have read a shared, whole-class play, *The Diary of Anne Frank,* accompanied by informational texts on the Holocaust, and the students have read a shared, whole-class novel (*The Giver, Haroun and*

**Photo 8.1** Partner reading: Da'Sha and Matt

*the Sea of Stories,* or *Waiting for the Rain,* depending on the class). And each student has read as part of a book club. Of course, exact timing depends on the quantity of short stories, poems, and articles; the length of the shared novel and play; the number of book club meetings; the amount of writing, standardized test preparation, and any additional components of the curriculum; and the skill and the fluency of the readers. We have read and responded together in class—as a class; in small groups; and, at times, individually—and students having been reading and responding daily as homework.

The student Reading Journals are bursting, and some students keep their Reading Journals Volume I in class crates at the back of the classroom as they embark on Volume II. Readers have experienced "journal-starter" responses, strategy responses, double-entry journals, sticky notes, poetry response, interactive and collaborative response, discussions, anticipatory response, abandonment response, evaluative responses, and text reformulations (see Chapter 9). My readers are ready to move to the next step: individual reading in class. This stage is what some might refer to as "Reading Workshop," although we have been using workshop format in our classes all year—with shared and book club texts. The students have been trained towards independence in their reading and their responding. Furthermore, by beginning with shared readings and progressing to book clubs, each class has built a reading and response *community.* By the time students are reading their own texts during class, they do not feel they are reading alone; they may be reading separately but not in isolation—individually, not independently.

My readers are now choosing their own books for in-class reading and discussions, but I am even now adding to their arsenal of reader response. I am continuing to guide them so that they can ultimately choose appropriate and effective ways to respond to their readings.

# READING LIKE A WRITER:
# AUTHOR'S CRAFT RESPONSES

At this point in the year, I alternate reading workshop with writing workshop; therefore, one of the elements I want readers to notice in their texts is author's craft. We read when we write, and my goal is to have readers notice writing when they read so they can become not only better readers but better writers. In other words, my students have been trained to read "like a reader," becoming cognizant of first *the* reading strategies and then *their* reading strategies. The next step is to guide them also to read "like a writer," to encourage them to become mindful of writing strategies, the goal being to apply these strategies to their writings when appropriate and effective. The author's craft lessons spotlight writing elements, such as figurative language, specific nouns and active verbs, point of view, dialogue, use of detail, as well as the ways in which authors craft story elements—all topics of their current writing workshop focus lessons. I might say something like, "Authors handle description in unique ways, but most employ certain writing techniques." For my demonstration, I read a passage, which is on the overhead. Then I continue, "Let's look at this text and see how Joan Bauer handles description in this excerpt from her novel *Hope Was Here*."

> That's when I saw the two-story white frame building with the bright red double stairways descending from the glass door—one from the left, one from the right. An American flag waving from a flagpole. A walk of flowering trees circled toward the back. Every window had a flower box packed with blossoms. Above the front porch hung a big sign: WELCOME STAIRWAYS. (2000/2002, p. 15)

I point out a writing strategy that Bauer has used. "I notice that the author uses specific details, such as "American flag," "flowering trees," "two-story white frame building," "glass door," "flower box *packed* with blossoms." I invite the students to contribute some specific details they noticed in the description. "Colors—red and white." "Double staircases." We notice that the author accomplishes description by using nouns and adjectives. We draw our visualizations, and as the pairs compare, they see that their drawings are remarkably similar. I point out that the more specific an author is, the more alike the visualizations will be from reader to reader.

I then provide an example of an excerpt from another novel, such as *Mistaken Identity* by Lisa Scottoline (1999/2002):

> The gym was in <u>North Philadelphia</u>, far from the glistening business district. Going north on <u>Broad Street</u>, the white marble of <u>City Hall</u> was replaced by the red plastic of <u>Kentucky Fried Chicken</u>, the dark glass of vacant storefronts, and the fake wood paneling of check-cashing agencies with lines around the corner, like opening day of a first-run movie. Unemployment was higher in this area and the evidence was on every street corner, where the homeless shook <u>McDonald's</u> cups of change. (p. 139)

In a guided practice, students highlight the specific details they find, especially proper nouns, and then we compare.

For one of their responses that week, students are asked to reflect on their author's craft of writing about the setting. I ask readers to apply this lesson to their independent reading and to notice how their authors write descriptions or introduce setting, especially if they employ the techniques that the two authors we analyzed used: specific details and explicit proper names for nouns (e.g., a glass of Pepsi, a bowl of Rice Krispies). As a response model, I show an example from my reading of Jordan Sonnenblick's *Notes from the Midnight Driver* (2006/2007).

---

Sonnenblick, Jordan, *Notes from the Midnight Driver*, pp. 43–44

*The room was standard hospital issue: white walls, off-white floor tiles, turkey/Lysol scent. It had no decorations whatsoever—no cards, no "Get Well" balloons, no family pictures. So the only thing I could possibly look at was the man on the bed. (pp. 43–44)*

I noticed that the images the author used to describe the nursing-home room (walls, floor, scent) were very realistic, and he used two senses to make it come alive—sight and smell. It was interesting how he combined the food aroma with the cleaning solution odor, which are the two smells I always notice in a hospital or nursing home.

Also effective was a description of not only what is there, but what is *not* there—cards, balloons, pictures—any evidence of caring. Sonnenblick creates the sad, lonely feeling of a nursing home by writing that there are "no decorations." The setting sets the tone.

I also liked the way the author transitions from the setting to the character, almost like "the man" is part of the setting and gradually morphs into a character.

---

As a guided practice, the students write a response to another description in class. I may even use an excerpt from the novel we read. They compare results with their neighbors.

Since I want to introduce the concept of responding to a writer's craft simply, at first I use a "Responses to Author's Craft" form (Resource B, #15), which asks readers to notice and "copy from your reading examples of *good writing*," focusing on a craft we have studied that week.

The next day in writing workshop, students can try to employ the techniques they noticed in their own writings, imitating one of the authors they read. We are integrating our two workshops through the focus lessons.

Whenever we have focus lessons throughout the year, I ask my students to respond to a particular focus "sometime during the week, *if* and *when* appropriate to your reading." I do not want my readers to apply a certain strategy that may not fit their reading, and they can only notice a technique when it actually occurs. For example, that night's reading may not include any description. They know that I will expect a focus response at some point, and since they are listing the focus lessons on their Daily Reading Log sheets, they can keep track.

As we progress through writing focus lessons and the students learn about various author crafts, their observations become cumulative, and the readers choose to what craft(s) they will respond, just as they now write about the reading strategies they actually are employing in their readings. Response becomes less artificial; it becomes more authentic and meaningful. The response form the students now use (Resource B, #16) is a more inclusive form requiring a combination of responses: a brief summary, a review of reading strategies, and response to writer's craft.

I model a response that combines a short summary, a recognition of my use of questioning and visualization reading strategies, and an analysis of the author's crafts of humor and using jargon based on the first 48 pages of *Hope Was Here* (see Figure 8.1).

---

**Figure 8.1**　Sample: Reading Strategies—Author's Craft Response Journal

Date: March 15, 2009　　　　　　　　　　　　　　　　Pages 1 to 41

Title: *Hope Was Here*　　　　　　　　　　　　　　　Author: Joan Bauer

**What I Read** (brief summary):

Seventeen-year-old Hope has always lived with her aunt. They move frequently, working in restaurants. Hope has worked as a waitress since she was 14 years old. They have just moved to Mulhoney, Wisconsin, where Addle is a cook in a diner and Hope is filling in as a waitress. The diner's owner, G. T. Stoop, has leukemia but has decided to run against the mayor, who always runs unopposed. Hope has just met the staff of the Welcome Stairways and served her first meal there.

**How I Read** (What reading strategies you used. Give specific examples from your book):

Since I just began the book, I had a lot of **questions.**

1. G. T. Stoop and the mayor definitely have a conflict. How will Hope be involved?

2. Hope has never met her father but keeps a scrapbook for him. Will he appear?

3. The other waitress doesn't seem to like Hope right away. Why?

I also have been trying to **visualize** the diner. There is a good description of the outside of the diner, and I have eaten in diners.

**How it was written** (What you noticed about writer's craft. Give specific examples from your book):

I noticed the author's use of **humor,** which I expected after hearing her speak at the conference in New York City. It's not laugh-out-loud funny but witty: "I've been sitting on the bench so long, I forgot how to play the game."

The story is written in **first-person POV,** so the reader knows what Hope is thinking. It is effective because she hasn't met or talked to many people yet, and this POV also helped to fill in her background.

Since the **setting** has been different restaurants, the author uses restaurant jargon and sometimes gives us the layperson's terms; for example a *short stack*, which is restaurant-speak for a small order of pancakes.

---

In his response to S. E. Hinton's novel *Tex*, pages 1–17, Lou, who had read at least two other S. E. Hinton novels, wrote the following journal:

What I read:

I just started reading a new book called *Tex*. I learned about the main character, Tex, and his brother and their father. Their father goes away for the summer and they have no more money left so Tex's

*(Continued)*

(Continued)

brother sells their horses. Tex loves his horses, especially Neghrito. Tex is determined to get the horse back no matter what the cost is. Tex also fights with his brother for selling his horses, and he loses and gets beat pretty bad.

How I read:

Since this is a new book, I asked a lot of questions and made some predictions:

I asked if this book was going to be the same as all of the author's other books. I also asked in what time period does it take place, and are there going to be any gang-related things in this book like the others?

I predicted that the book is going to be about gangs but just in another town. This book is not like the others, though. So far I haven't heard [read] anything about gangs. I don't know if I am going to like this book as much as I did the other ones, but I need to read more to find out.

How it was written:

The author's craft is the same, mostly, just like all of S. E. Hinton's books are. They are very detailed when action scenes happen, like when Tex and his older brother are fighting, she describes the pain and what broke and how the room looked after they fought. She described the pain and the swelling on Tex's face too. She almost makes you feel like the character and it's happening to someone you know.

Even though Lou had read only 17 pages of the novel, from this journal entry I can tell first of all that Lou did read and, then, that he understood the exposition (the main characters, the setting, the initial situation, and the protagonist's motivation for decisions he will make and actions he will take). Lou, as a reader, is making connections from this novel to other texts and, based on those connections, is asking questions and making predictions. He even predicts that this book will be different and, because of this, that he may not like it in the same way, but he's determined to give it a chance. Importantly for Lou as an emerging writer, he is noticing not just detail but the type of details authors include, such as how the room looked after they fought. The next step is for students to write this type of information on sticky notes as they read and then to include actual examples in their response journals, as discussed in Chapter 4. My readers are now beginning to read like writers and, as writers, are writing for readers.

## CHOICE READING—CHOICE RESPONSE

The Reading Strategies—Author's Craft form is the final teacher-created form that I use. My students now have the training to choose an appropriate response. In most cases, the scaffolding can be removed. Many students, however, choose to continue using the forms; they feel safer retaining structure. At this point during my first year of using reader response, students asked me to make available copies of all the forms we had used that year. I bought a divided shelf unit in which I placed copies. I found that some students took forms each day, some took forms on some days, and some never used the forms again. Readers who still used the forms made use of double-entry journals some days and author-craft journals on others. I found that even those who still used form journals were making decisions on how, when, and what to use, depending on their needs and their texts. They were applying the lessons of the year by self-directing their responses. Students who were not writing on forms were synthesizing the techniques facilitated by the forms; they showed that they had internalized the process of response.

## MULTIGENRE RESPONSE

I found that readers were still responding in poetry when fitting. At this point, I encourage my students to respond in different genres, such as news articles, eulogies for characters, or scripts, but ones that are appropriate to their readings. One student's creativity illustrates just how effective this variety in genre can be. We had read and acted a play in class, and Ceire applied the genre we had studied to her independent reading but in a way in which it dramatically interpreted and illustrated her reaction to the text she was reading:

For One More Day Response 2

I have not gotten too far into the book and I already hate Chick's dad. He's a pig. I hate the part where he is telling Chick's mom that his ziti isn't right. That she didn't cook it right. If *my* step-dad said it to *my* mom, it would go a little something like this:

[Mary (mom), Bob (step-dad), Hanna (little sister-7), Bobby (little brother-10), and Ceire (14) all sitting at the table in the dining room. The ziti is in the middle of the table and Bob reaches over to serve himself. He puts a scoop of it on his plate, then Bobby's and then Hanna's. Ceire and Mary serve themselves. Bob takes his first mouthful and makes a disgusted face. He drops his fork, and it rings against the glass plate. Mary looks at him with a fierce expression.]

Bob [*angrily*]: This is all wrong. You didn't make this right. There is something wrong with the cheese or the oil or something.

Mary [*calmly*]: Oh, sorry.

[Mary rises from the table with a blank expression on her face. She walks over to Bob, grabs his plate and carries it to the kitchen. She scrapes the ziti into the trashcan and washes the plate in the sink. She puts the plate in the dishwasher and walks upstairs. Ceire, Bobby, and Hanna are trying to hide smiles. They look down at their plates and continue eating without looking up or saying a word. Bob is shifting uncomfortably in his seat. Mary comes down moments later with a pillow and a small blanket. She walks into the family room and throws them on the couch. She returns to her seat at the table and smiles at Bobby.]

Mary *[cheerily]:* So how was school today, sweetie?

Bobby *[trying to fight his laughter]:* Uhh . . . good. Can I have a snack?

Mary: Sure.

[Bobby and Bob both rise at the same time. Bob turns behind him and walks down to the basement. Bobby walks into the kitchen. Mary resumes talking with Ceire and Hannah.]

## DRAWING AS RESPONSE

Photo 8.2   Carlin drawing, Steph reading

Some students have trouble with words; they see and describe their readings more readily as pictures. Many readers comprehend by means of visualization—their images are based on the author's descriptions. In visualization responses, I request that the students supply the text that led to the visualization, either as Sarah did (see Figure 8.2) or by labeling their drawings with words from the text.

However, other readers draw their responses because they are comparing reading their text to viewing a movie. Or some students, especially our English-language learner (ELL) students, find it easier to communicate in pictures than in words. I have had a few students who successfully executed certain journal responses as graphics. This strategy works best with summarizations.

Using drawings to retell a story, a chapter, or a section of a book—whether fiction or nonfiction, is more than simply summarizing events. It is synthesization, and from the drawings, I can understand and evaluate how and if the reader comprehends the text. Even more valuable, when artists review their own drawings, they literally see if they have omitted any essential information or lost the sequencing of events. The graphic novel adaptation by Antony Johnston of *Stormbreaker* by Anthony Horowitz would be one model to show students, as well as any of the graphic Classics Illustrated. None of the graphic depictions replace reading the originals, but they provide good summaries, as well as sharing the tone and some of the language of the original text.

Katie's graphic depiction reveals her understanding and interpretation of the final chapter of Salman Rushdie's *Haroun and the Sea of Stories,* a novel that readers always agree is very visual (see Figure 8.3).

**Figure 8.2**    Sample: Sarah's Visualization

Drawing can be more than visualization. I noticed that when I ask students to draw what they see, the pictures can differ dramatically. And if I ask them to draw what they *read*, some draw symbolically. When my students read Daniel Keyes's short story "Flowers for Algernon," I asked them to represent Charlie Gordon and his world before and after the operation that increased his IQ by 300 percent. One student used a picture of a plain square to symbolize Charlie's uncomplicated thinking at an IQ of 68 and an intricate geometric shape of many colors to demonstrate the complexity of his cognition at 208. Other readers drew more literal representations. Readers' pictorial responses are as varied as their verbal reflections and give me more information about my students as readers.

**Figure 8.3** Sample: Katie's *Haroun and the Sea of Stories* Chapter 12 Drawing

# REACHING THE GOAL: UNIQUE, VARIED, PERSONAL, INDIVIDUAL RESPONSE

As students read and respond throughout the year, their responses do not necessarily become longer, but they do become deeper and more meaningful, two of my goals for this program. Lacey, a very bright student and a strong reader, began the year reading *The DaVinci Code*. In one of her first responses, she shares her reactions to the plot:

> I felt nervous when Silas entered Teabing's home. I got all caught up in the emotion of the story and I was worried something bad was going to happen. Usually when I read, I get caught up with whatever is happening. I tend to either fall in love with the characters or hate them.

Instead of showing us that she gets "caught up in the emotion of the story," Lacey tells us. Her entry contains only one inference, *I felt. . . .*

In her next entry, she activates prior knowledge:

> When Sophie figured out that the language written on the vase was actually Leonardo DaVinci's backward English language, it reminded me of Mr. Scott. He was the first person to tell me about how DaVinci used to write his notes backwards in his journal so that nobody could read them.

In another entry, Lacey makes a text-to-self connection:

> When Sophie figured out her name was Greek for "wisdom," it reminds me of what I am studying in Humanities right now. I just recently found out that my name was English and that it came from a French nobleman's surname.

And then a text-to-text connection:

> When the narrator described the church, it reminded me of the Hogwart's castle in the book *Harry Potter*. The church was described as being really old. The church had gargoyles, knights, and many other scary things.

In her journal at the beginning of the year, Lacey demonstrates that she is using her Response Starters form and using reading strategies, but later in the year, it all comes together, and her responses become more unique and immediate, showing that she is transacting with the text. Contrast the September entries to her March responses to the novel *Stones in the Water* by Donna Jo Napoli.

In an early response to the book, Lacey activates prior knowledge *and* builds on it:

> While I was reading *Stones in the Water*, all of the research and work that I had done earlier in the year on the Holocaust came back—those stories about the concentration camps and the laws that were made. It was so sad that one man, one man, could have so much control. One thing I didn't know was how bad it was in Italy.

In her letter to one of the novel's characters, Lacey summarizes, points out important details, questions, infers, makes connections, and monitors her comprehension. As we read her letter, we almost forget that Roberto is a character in a book. We can see that Lacey has come to care about him as she told us in September she would; she even comforts him over his friend's death.

> Dear Roberto,
>
> I cannot believe the things that you have had to endure over the past few months. They are outrageous. You must be emaciated since you haven't been able to eat a proper meal in many months. I still cannot believe that Samuel (Enzo) dies. That is so sad, but I think that everything happens for a reason. If he hadn't died, you probably wouldn't have left the work camp. You would have continued working because you hoped that they would eventually set everyone free. You needed Samuel's death because it gave you that push you needed. He's now with you in spirit, and he's in a much better place. Aren't you lucky that Maurzio wanted to help you? He needed a favor, so, in return, he helped you out. He fed you, protected you from the Nazis, and helped you find your way home. Well, maybe not. I was a little confused at the end because it never stated that you wanted to go home, and I thought that was a little odd. If I was in your position, I would want to get home ASAP. You hadn't seen your parents in months so I'm sure they wanted to see you. They probably thought that you were dead, but they would have been surprised to see you still breathing. I still can't believe you survived those terrible conditions. God clearly wanted you to live!
>
> Sincerely, Lacey

In another novel response, Lacey catalogs Roberto's character traits, supporting her opinions with quotes from the text and then elaborating with her own explanations, a technique she acquired from the double-entry journals. One example is when she writes that Roberto is "generous."

> Quote, pg. 58: "Eat half and I'll eat half and we can trade."
>
> Explanation: Somebody at the work camp had figured out that Samuel (Enzo) was Jewish. They threatened to tell his secret to the Nazis if Samuel didn't give the kid his food. Samuel had to cooperate. Roberto, being a very nice friend, from then on split his meals with Samuel.

One of her last responses to the novel merges text-to-text, text-to-self, and text-to-world connections, and Lacey shows the significance of the comparison:

> When Roberto finished building a concentration camp at his work camp, the Nazis filled it with Jewish people who were going to be killed. This reminded me of Anne Frank's story because she and her family were thrown into a concentration camp where they were either sent to work or killed. There was a difference, though. The concentration camp in the book didn't separate the men and women. They were put together because the camp was so small. The camp Anne Frank went to was separated *which meant she had to leave her dad* [emphasis added].

Lacey not only shows insight in her responses, she has assumed control of her own responding, another goal of the response program. She demonstrates this in her letters to authors—praise to Donna Jo Napoli and admonishment to Gregory Maguire for his *Mirror, Mirror:*

> I guess I had higher expectations, and this book did not come close to meeting them. . . . What kind of ending was that anyway! To me the ending is supposed to be the grand finale of the book and also wrap the story up. Your ending did not do either of those things.

She sympathizes with Julius Caesar (*Pharaoh*) over his death ("I can't believe that people that you had called your friends killed you.") and shows admiration of Cleopatra over hers:

> You tried desperately to fight for your children's lives. I really admire the way that you died. I would have hoped that I would have done the same thing. Your family mattered the most to you, and you were willing to kill yourself so that your children would be able to live. That is so brave and motherly. I hope to God that I will some day possess that same love for my children.

And even *Othello*'s Iago did not escape without a tongue, or rather pen, lashing. After she enumerates his villainies, Lacey admonishes, "You are truly an evil man, and I hope that the officers in Venice have taken care of you. Not that it matters now anyway; almost everyone's life has been ruined because of you."

Lacey's journal responses show creativity, variety, and her thinking processes as she reads. Her journal illustrates how her reading and responding has transformed over the year as scaffolding is set up and then removed once the structure is in place—she is not only reading individually but responding in her own highly personal, distinctive way.

By the time students are reading individually in the class reading workshop, they can choose and vary the ways in which they want to respond. At this point, readers have been trained to express their own unique, immediate, spontaneous impressions and are transacting with the text in a variety of ways. As I respond to their journals, in notes on the journal pages or in conferences as they read, I encourage them to read more deeply.

# A SAMPLE JOURNAL FOR ONE NOVEL

Ceire typically read a novel every two weeks. Therefore, within two weeks, her responses went from an anticipation response, through the book, to an evaluation response. Her journal contained questions, connections to other texts, personal reflections, predictions, responses to author's craft, and specific details as support. Through her journals, I discovered the novels, Ceire as a reader, and even Ceire as an individual. I saw her wrestling with comprehension, making inferences, and coming to conclusions on her own. I did not have to have read the book to follow her reasoning, but if I had, I sometimes included questions for her to think about. Many times, based on student responses, I can volunteer additional background information about the book or the author or recommend other books the reader might enjoy. The journal becomes a dialogue.

Ceire's two-week journal reveals her thinking and reactions as she selected, read, and evaluated *Twisted* by Laurie Halse Anderson:

Response 1: Why I Chose This Book & Anticipation Response

I chose this book for basically the same reasons I chose Speak. I am very fond of the author and I have heard so many excellent things about the book. It is also going be the second book I can mark off of my "Books To Read List," so it's accomplishing a goal I set for myself. When I first saw the book I wanted to read it because of the cover art. The twisted pencil looks very cool and somewhat real, so it caught my eye. Reading the first few pages, I immediately noticed something that makes this book different from the other Anderson books I have read. The main character is a boy. It also sounds like he has gotten into some trouble since he mentions a court order for community service, which involves fixing up his school's (George Washington High) roof. I believe his parents have a troubled marriage because he said that they had just gotten back from their therapy session. There is still that sarcastic sense of humor that I expected from Ms. Anderson. I wonder what crazy twist she will throw at me this time? (Ha-ha, that was kind of a pun!)

Response 2: pages 1 to 41

I really like this book. I've always read books that are told from a girl perspective, so I'm getting a taste of what guys think about stuff. By stuff, I mean girls, what they notice about them, how they react, what they notice—basically what Seventeen magazine says they tell you on page 52, but with a more sarcastic tone. In way I sort of knew some of the guy point of view because I grew up with a bunch of guys. It's different from the book though, because you are getting the whole opinion, even the stuff my friends probably left out. The one thing I like about this book is that the most beautiful and popular girl is not a cheerleader for once. It is a volleyball player, a preppy sport, but at least it's different from every other book and movie about high school. Tyler really seems to have a crush on this girl, Bethany Miller. According to him she's a "Goddess." I wonder if he has a shot with her. He is clearly out of his league but he has changed a lot over the summer, so that could work to his advantage. His major disadvantage would be that her brother, Chip, beat him every day in middle school and her father is his father's boss. He goes to a party with his family that is held by the Millers and ends up sending Bethany and himself to the hospital in need of stitches. It wasn't really his fault though because Chip pushed him into Bethany who then fell into a waiter carrying glass champagne glasses.

Response 3: Purpose-for-Reading Response

I am extremely eager to find out what the first day of senior year will be like for Tyler! He has gotten a lot more muscular and manlier, I guess you could say. He also knows he can take Chip and all his friends, and they know it too. And to top it all off, he is friends with the most popular girl in school, who just happens to be his crush. However, the teachers are bound to give him a hard time because of the graffiti he wrote on the walls of the school last year as a prank. I wonder how the principal will treat him. There is probably going to be a plethora of absolutely insane rumors going around about him, too. I'm sure glad I'm not him!

Response 4: pages 42 to 155

I was completely sucked into the book! I literally could not put it down. A lot has happened in this hour of reading. Bethany makes it clear the she like him, and he has no idea what to do with himself. At the football game Tyler suddenly kisses her, and she kisses back. She later asks him to go the Halloween party hosted by one of the rich and popular kids from school. Since he has no ride and no car, he walks to the party, and it takes him two hours. By the time he gets there, Bethany is completely inebriated (ha-ha, our new vocabulary word), and she and Tyler almost have sex. Luckily Tyler's "brain kicked in" and he knew it was wrong to do that while she was drunk. Bethany takes this the wrong way completely and says that he doesn't like her so he blew her off. She disappeared and he didn't find her until everybody was kicked out. He had to carry her to her brother's car and drove Chip, Parker (Chip's friend) and Bethany home because they were all wasted. A few days later something horrible happened. Laurie never ceases to amaze me with her outrageous twists. Pictures of Bethany showed up on the Internet, and she was naked. The police, the school, and his parole officer immediately accused Tyler. He knew he didn't do it but he was still seen as guilty by the student body. Horrible rumors were going around about him and Chip hates him more than ever. Bethany hasn't been in school for days, I hope she is somewhat okay. There are plenty of rumors about her, too. I hope she realizes that Tyler didn't do it and they can still be friends. And Tyler's dad has gone psycho. I don't like him at all. His parents need to divorce; they are only trying to stay together because of the kids. As far as I am concerned, you're hurting the kids. His dad is a jerk, a total and complete jerk. I hope Hannah and Yoda will be there for him. I hope Bethany comes to school soon.

## Response 5: Character-Trait Response

Tyler has a very low self-esteem, but he is also courageous. He talks about what other people see him as a lot, which I consider low esteem. But he also has the guts to challenge Chip, the guy who made him miserable his whole life, so that counts for something.

Yoda is a sweet nerd. He's way too into video games and Star Wars, but he so sweet to Hannah and her friends.

Chip is an egotistical, butt-headed bully. He's so concerned with beating kids up so he can look cool in front of his friends. I hate people like that. And he always cries to Daddy for help when things get too rough. Seriously he needs to grow up.

Tyler's dad is just a jerk. He is never there for his family, screams at his wife and Tyler's constantly. He is just looking for a scapegoat, and that seems to be Tyler.

Hannah is a very active and feisty. She is a very aggressive field hockey player, and she hates it when her brother tells her what to do. I'd say she is the stereotype teenage girl.

Tyler's mom also possesses low self-esteem. She should stick up for herself more around her husband and stop making up excuses for his irrational behavior. She should get a divorce; that's what she needs to do.

Bethany is kind and sassy. She is very bubbly and flirtatious but isn't the stereo-type popular girl that constantly puts people down.

## Response 6: pages 156 to 200

Bethany showed up to school. It wasn't the best day for her, but her parents forced her to go. Tyler wasn't allowed to even be in the same room as Bethany anymore. I was getting so mad; these constant interviews with the police are getting annoying. He didn't do it; just because he had a run in with the law before doesn't me he would sexually harass the girl of his dreams. These couple chapters were extremely twisted. First, Tyler was jumped by Chip and two of his friends. The funny thing is that they had to cover his face up while they did it. What scaredy-cats. Tyler also tried to kill himself. I was so sick when I read that. He envisioned his funeral like he looked forward to it. The sad thing is there are actually kids out there who think like that. Sometimes the world, when read through a book, can help us understand the world that we live in.

Response 7: pages 200–242

There were two amazing parts of this book; I was so happy and excited when I read them. The first is that Tyler stood up to Chip in a major way. He threw the pink blanket that was used to cover up his face (while he was getting beat up) back at Chip. It was great. Chip was all "Get out of here before I flatten you" and "Right here, right now, loser." Then Tyler said, "Bravo, very good. Ask me to fight in the room that has the most security." Before he left, Tyler told Chip that if he goes crying to Daddy to have him call one of his lawyers. I was laughing and clapping. I said, "Go, Tyler!" out loud and didn't realize it until my dad started laughing. It was a little embarrassing. The second is that he stood up to his dad. This was more drastic and freaky though. He went down in the basement (after his dad basically blamed all of his life's problems on him) to straighten things out. Oh yeah, he brought a baseball bat with him. He said a few things to him before he went ballistic and completely destroyed the train set that his dad spent year's working on. I thought his dad would go insane and beat him, but he didn't. Everything was calm and kind of awed. He calmly explained to him and his mother that he almost killed himself. It was so heartbreaking. It was a very strange conversation, but in a good way. Besides the whole "I almost killed myself' thing," I think it was just strange because the things that were said needed to be said a very long time ago.

Response 8: Cause-and-Effect Response

I think this whole book was just one big cause and effect. Every book is, but this was basically set off by one event. Well, kind of. Tyler was a dork his whole life (cause) and he was tired of it. So, he decided to pull a prank so that he would be remembered (effect). He got caught and was sentenced to community service (effect). The work made him gain muscle and strength enough to beat up Chip (effect). From there everything just goes on. There are plenty of other examples of this relationship I could give but, in my opinion, they are all caused by him getting taken away by the police. This reputation got him into a lot of trouble but it also got him a lot of things he wanted at the same time.

Response 9: Point-of-View Response

The book is told through first person point of view by Tyler. It affects the story because it's being told through the eyes of a "loser." It is what made the story so great. It shows how hard the transition from complete nerd to jock can be. Actually, it shows how much the desire to be noticed or remembered can affect somebody. The story could have been told through Chip's eyes or Bethany's or Hannah's but that would not have captured the emotion that Tyler shows throughout the whole book. Tyler told the story and if he didn't, the story would have been horrible and I would not have read it. That is the short version of the point I'm trying to get across.

Response 10: Finishing-A-Book Evaluation

AMAZING! I like this book better than Speak. It is so good. The whole time I read this book I was thinking of this MTV show called High School Stories: Scandals, Pranks and Controversies. It is one of my favorite shows. This is the only book by Laurie Halse Anderson I've read that's told through a guy's point of view. There is still that sarcastic wit and unpredictable twist that makes her books so amazingly amazing, though. The thing I liked about this story is that it's really not that far-fetched. The whole part with Bethany Millbury's photos is a little out there, but not totally unbelievable. There are some sick people out there. (Sick kids, too!) I am not saying that I agree with kids who want to kill themselves or even seriously think about it, but I think I understand why they would a little better. I mean, Tyler is right; when you go to a funeral you feel bad about all the stuff you said and did that was mean to the person who is dead. It was a sad book, but not the sad that makes you want to be sorry. It was the kind of sad that makes you angry and anxious and makes your chest tight all at the same time. I'm not sure if that made sense, but I don't know how I could put it into words. Definitely a good book—recommending it to everybody who bothers to listen when I tell them about yet another book I've read.

Ceire's journal entries appear to be more than "five-minute responses," but she typed them after she read and retained them on a file that she printed out to add to her journal; they might actually have only taken five minutes or so to write. Some students find that they have longer responses because they enjoy writing about their novels or their reading and like to have someone to read their musings; they recognize that they have my undivided attention for at least a few minutes each week.

# ADAPTATIONS

Since at this point, the readers have six months' instruction in response choice and the groundwork and training to make those choices, they self-adapt. They have experienced a gradual release program of modeling, guided practices, and application of response strategies and skills. Those who still feel they need the safety net of the forms use them; those who are able and willing to take off on their own do so. Students appreciate that I even now monitor them by reading their journals each week so they cannot stray too far off course. Most importantly, through all the lessons and models, they realize the purpose and importance of their responses and understand the goals of reader response, and by now they feel more confident.

Flocks of geese fly in a *V* formation that is believed to improve overall fluid dynamics. This is known as "drafting" and helps the geese save energy and permits them to fly longer distances. Flying in a *V* also has social advantages: it allows birds to communicate with each other while on the wing. The formation is cooperative, not competitive, because the birds take advantage of the situation, not each other. In the classroom, modeling and working together help the struggling readers gain confidence by implementing "drafting," letting weaker students glide on the "wind" of others as students converse and then meet in small groups and book clubs. The concept of drafting, as I apply it in my classroom, gives all students turns to ride the wind and to lead the group. We have spent two-thirds of the year "drafting."

As an adaptation for further drafting, I encourage reluctant or struggling readers to choose books to read with a partner during individual reading. I have two copies of most of the books in my library, and if not, the school library or another teacher usually has a copy. There are also book club sets that two or three students might like to read, even though we are not meeting in formal book clubs; this arrangement functions as a mini club where students can choose to read at the same time and meet for a few minutes every few reading days to discuss their books. These readers may choose to write their responses as letters to each other.

Even when students are reading individually, they meet in small groups from time to time to compare plots, characters, setting, and authors, especially when I see trends through their responses. Teachers can institute an author study through which a group of students reads different books written by the same author. I have offered author studies as an option but not a requirement, since I want students to have as much choice as possible at this time of the year.

Every once in a while, readers who have abandoned forms slip back into writing short summaries or "shorthand" responses ("I was surprised." "John has low self-esteem."). When this happens, we design simple logos, such as an eye for visualization, to identify their thinking or strategies. Reviewing responses and labeling them in this way usually prompts readers to dig deeper. An even simpler way is to ask students to return to the past week's response and highlight their Response Starters. Students usually realize that they have only retold their reading. As all year, my expectations for readers of varying strengths differ as I observe their reactions to what they read, and I can offer them differentiated instruction by my responses. It is important that they become stronger and more analytical in terms of their capabilities.

## The Case of Julio, ELL Student

Julio was an ELL student. He moved to the United States during the first quarter of eighth grade, speaking Spanish and knowing very little English. At first I gave him very simple books—picture dictionaries and high-interest, low-reading nonfiction texts—but I wanted to make him a member of our reading community as soon as possible. As a whole-class, shared text, my class read *The Giver* by Lois Lowery. I chose this novel from the selection of classroom sets because it was available in Spanish. I felt that if Julio read the same novel we were reading, he would be able to follow, even profit from, our classroom discussions and possibly at times be able to contribute. He was asked to respond to his reading in Spanish or through drawings until he knew more English. He could even share his picture interpretations with other class members, drawing being a universal language. I also suggested that Julio make a list of the words in English that he knew or was learning (or that he looked up in a translation dictionary). I found that he listened intently to our class or small-group discussions, which were based on the students' response sheets and, toward the end of the novel, he sometimes felt confident enough to join in.

By the time the class moved into book clubs, Julio was ready and motivated to progress to an English-language text. When the students chose book clubs, I recommended that Julio join the group who selected *The Pigman* by Paul Zindel. In past years, I had used this novel as a whole-class text and knew that it was a high-interest story with a relatively simple vocabulary and plot. I also knew that the students in that particular group would be tolerant and supportive of Julio's efforts to contribute to the discussions. Another reason for endorsing *The Pigman* was that I had discovered a chapter-by-chapter synopsis of the novel online, which I translated into Spanish. That way, Julio could read the summary before reading a chapter. Not only did I observe Julio contributing to the club discussions, I noticed him leading a few of them. His English, both speaking and reading, increased dramatically, as did his writing skills. While he still responded frequently in Spanish, he then translated those responses for me, thereby adding to his vocabulary and writing skills. He told me that he was beginning to think in English when responding to the novel. By the time the students were reading individually in reading workshop, Julio was also choosing his own texts and responses.

# PART III

## After-Reading Response

# 9

## Post-Reading Response

### TEXT REFORMULATION

"I'm finished," Jen said, slamming her book shut. She ran back to the classroom library to put the book back on the shelf and grab another, promptly forgetting the novel just read. No looking back, no reflecting on the text as a whole. She wrote and drew responses to individual segments as she read, so I couldn't say that she hadn't thought about any of the book. But now she felt it was time to move on. It was the "I came, I read, I conquered," philosophy. "The End" meant the end.

*The whole is greater than the sum of its parts,* I recited to myself from rote. I couldn't remember the source of the quote, but it certainly seemed to fit this situation. I thought about my doctors. My cardiologist looks and responds to the function of my heart (response to Chapter 1). The dermatologist reacts to the damage the sun has left behind on my skin (Chapter 2). Gastroenterologists study tests to explain my heartburn (Chapter 3), and there's the endocrinologist who checks my thyroid and cholesterol (Chapters 4–5). Thank goodness, though, for the internist who looks back on *all* my complaints, tests, and responses of my specialists and reflects on the entity as a whole.

I had noticed a lot of books closing immediately after our shared novel also, the students too eager to hand them in and move on. However, after students read, it is important for them to return to the text and interact with it to become skilled and reflective readers. This is true for both nonfiction and fictional texts, although the benefits for interacting with content area texts are more obvious—learning, comprehending, using, and mastering material.

I cannot overstate the importance and advantages of returning to the text for comprehension and interpretation. Lucy Calkins in *The Art of Teaching Reading* (2001) wrote,

> When a child has a keen sense of what is important about the whole plot and how the details reflect the big ideas, and when she has the chance to talk through her ideas, her interpretation will be the strongest. (p. 486)

She also states, "By working with students to view a text in light of the overall interpretation they have proposed, we can help them develop a sense of what it is like to open up an entirely new layer within a story" (p. 479). Like many others, I find that every time I reread a book, I create expanded, enhanced, and even more innovative interpretations, making the text more interesting. Students notice this too and tell me, "I learned more this time," or "I never noticed *that*." I like the simple way a colleague of mine phrased it: "Literature doesn't kiss on the first date."

But how can we encourage students to return to the text and to respond to the writing as a whole? Many teachers might answer this challenge with a test. I have never believed in testing the book. First of all, students study their notes or past responses, not grasping what they missed or looking for deeper meaning; instead they look for test-type details. Also, while it would be possible to prepare a test for a shared text or even book club reading, it is impossible to create tests for readers' divergent independent choice readings. Besides the obvious need for assessments, the importance of post-reading activities is to move students beyond literal understanding of text.

I have often heard presenters and teachers criticize after-reading projects by stating, "When I finish a book, *I* don't make a diorama." This is true. However, as reflective readers, we do sit back and consider or discuss with others our reading and the significance of what the author has said. We mull over the text, compare notes with other readers, and mentally contrast the text with other texts, either written by the same author or other writers. Sometimes we compare the book with a movie based on the book. When I finish a book, I may not build a project out of materials, but I do create one in my mind. And that is what we need to do as teachers; we need to train our students to return to texts to question, interpret, compare, and analyze. This process starts in school and becomes internalized as students become highly skilled readers.

I have found that the best way to encourage students to return to the text is to ask them, as their after-reading response, to transform the text into a different format. Each rereading of a text gives readers a greater and deeper understanding, making them better readers and increasing comprehension. Other advantages of these activities are learning and using role-playing, inferring, and questioning techniques.

> As students worked through their reformulations, they returned to the text, reread portions, argued over meanings, questioned whether something was important or not, and listened to each other's interpretations. Text reformulation encourages dependent readers to think critically about the text without overwhelming them. The teacher never has to tell students to "find the main idea" or "make an inference"; students simply do these things while working on their reformulations. As students begin the process of reformulating, they must analyze and evaluate not only the text but also the writing they are creating about the text. (Beers, 2003, p.162)

This synthesis uses complex cognitive skills, even involving evaluation as students decide what to include and how. As Stephanie Harvey and Anne Goudvis (2000) said, all such activities "involve putting together assorted parts to make a new whole, which is what synthesizing is all about" (p. 146). David Booth (2001) built on their thinking when he wrote, "When we synthesize, we change what we thought we knew; we expand our personal understanding. We move from recounting the information into rethinking our own constructs of the world" (p. 37).

I have found, as have Irene C. Fountas and Gay Su Pinnell (2000), that projects work best when students

- are highly engaged in text over time.
- have learned a great deal through discussion and analysis.
- know how to use the different modes of expression that are available to them.
- select their own format in which to present their knowledge. (p. 288)

One activity, particularly successful with whole-class shared novels, is a trial, a multidimensional, high-interest activity. When asking students to work on or consider the choice of a trial, I first discuss trial terms, techniques, strategies, and procedures. Most students have watched enough law and crime shows on television to be familiar with the format. The class practices with a revised, slightly more impartial version of "Goldilocks and the Three Bears" that I created for this purpose. They determine the witnesses, arguments, and evidence. Since students are working with a modified version of the tale, they return to the text to look for or check "facts." However, the text is familiar enough that they can complete the task in a class period or two. The students do not actually perform the trial, but they list witnesses, arguments, and evidence and write their opening statements, which delineate their arguments.

In a full-fledged trial experience, after reading *The Pigman* by Paul Zindel, one class charged the protagonists, John and Lorraine, with contributing to the death of Mr. Pignati in a civil case. The class divided into prosecution and defense teams to prepare and present the trial, a reformulation of the text. Likewise, students who read Elizabeth Speare's *The Witch of Blackbird Pond* charged Kit, their protagonist, with the practice of witchcraft in a criminal case. Students in smaller groups have transformed Poe's short stories into trials. If the entire class has not read the text, the remaining students can serve as an impartial jury. Sometimes I am surprised at the novels, such as Naomi Shahib Nye's *Habibi*, in which the students discover legal issues.

After *The Pigman* trial, students responded to a few questions about the reformulation experience:

Question: How did you learn to do your part in the trial?

Answer 1: "I learned to do my part in the trial by re-reading the zookeeper's part in the book and envisioning it in my own way and by putting it into my own words that would, hopefully, result in positive effects for the defensive side."—Dianne

Question: What thinking skills do you think you used?

Answer 1: "I used analysis and evaluation to try to decide what type of jury it was and what kinds of arguments might make them vote for the Prosecution."—Kris

Answer 2: "The thinking skills I used were analyzing and reading between the lines [inferring]."—Matt

Question: How did you make decisions? How did your team make decisions?

Answer 1: "I made my decisions by thinking what I would have been asked if it were me who committed the so-called crime. And my team and I made decisions by talking and thinking things out together. Mainly teamwork."—Stacy

Another activity that works well with any size group (triad, book clubs, or whole class) is the novel newspaper. The goal is to create a newspaper based on the text. Of course, this is most effective if students are familiar with news writing, but they can always refer to a local newspaper. For demonstration purposes, I model a newspaper on a narrative poem with which the class has become familiar over the year, "Casey at the Bat." As guided practice, the class divides into small groups of two or three students each. The class is given another long narrative poem, such as "The Walrus and the Carpenter," which they read together, or a short story with which they are already familiar from a previous shared reading and a handout of news article formats (Resource B, #17). For practice, they create the front page of a newspaper, naming the paper and drafting three or four articles of different types based on the world of their text. If time for practice is short, students can list the types of articles they would use, draft the headlines, and list the "facts" from the text that they would include in each article. The trial and the newspaper projects serve as "twofers," since they also review persuasive and information writing.

Other types of individual or small-group reformulations are character scrapbooks or diaries, alphabet books, comic strips (photocopied onto transparencies, they can be shared with the class), picture books, or puppet shows; the ideas are limited only by students' creativity. Reformulation projects can also be more active and lend themselves better to groups of readers or book club members. Such activities include skits, in which participants reenact three or four pivotal scenes as a narrator connects the scenes; plays or musicals if a larger group is involved; talk shows; or interviews with a host as facilitator, the author, the publisher, a literary critic, and a reader. For a "brown bag" project, a group of readers, such as a book club, may present objects significant to the story by chapters or objects important to individual characters. I find that the brown bag project suits diverse abilities, because the more concretely minded students choose objects that actually appear in the text while the more abstract thinkers present representative objects.

One of my childhood memories resulted in a *This Is Your Life* show based on a past television program where people from the contestant's past appeared and talked about the contestant when they knew him. Then they spent a few minutes catching up. After I explained this idea to my students, a few groups took the idea and ran with it. Creating

**Photo 9.1**    A talk show presentation based on their novel: Anthony, Andrew, and Alayna

the show involved a range of cognitive skills. Participants had to predict who would come from the future to talk with and about the character and what they would say by looking back on the situation in the novel. It turned out to be a very reflective project.

One high school group I taught read *Oliver Twist* and staged their reformulation as a telethon for missing children. As they advised the listeners (the audience) of researched facts on missing children, reporters called in with updates on Oliver's whereabouts and predicaments. At a middle school level, this project could be adapted to a book such as *Monkey Island* by Paula Fox, which focuses on the plight of the homeless.

Some of the more innovative students have created interactive presentations involving audience members who have not read the book. One of my book clubs read *The War Between the Classes* by Gloria Miklowitz and, as their presentation, gave each audience member a colored armband and put the class through short exercises based on the book's premise.

When the class brainstorms reformulation ideas, dioramas have never appeared on the initial lists; however, one book club specifically asked to present a diorama-type project. They read Katherine Paterson's *Lyddie* and wanted to make models of the three settings—family cabin, Cutler's Tavern, and the factory in Lowell—because they thought that the settings were the vehicle that would advance their narration of the story most effectively. As skilled readers, we may not run out and make dioramas after reading a book, but we visualize the settings and evaluate their influence on the plot or, as in this case, the characters.

Besides compelling readers to reconsider text on another level, reformulations, which are much shorter than the text, give readers a way to share their books with the other students in the class. When students make presentations to their classmates, I tell them that the incentive is not the grade; it is the sharing of the novel with their classmates. I downplay the grade and assure them they will receive an A for a carefully planned and executed project; I also keep the rubric simple so that all can easily succeed. In other words, the grade should not drive the project, although it can be the motivation to complete the project and present it well. This sharing helps other readers make choices for future readings, and in this way, reading leads to more reading.

---

**Ideas for Reformulation**

- "Issue" talk show with characters
- Skit (scenes) with or without narrator
- Reality shows
- Mock trial
- Brown bag objects—by chapter or character
- Puppet show
- Radio interview with author, reader, publisher, historian
- *This Is Your Life* (Protagonist)
- Choral reading of a narrative poem of the story
- Movie trailers
- Newspaper of world of the novel
- Picture books, ABC books, graphic books
- Character scrapbooks
- Narrative poetry retellings of novels
- Powerpoint presentations

Another purpose for text reformulation is as a vehicle for review. My language arts class had finished reading Lois Lowry's novel *The Giver* and was preparing to write a persuasive essay based on the book. As a quick review, I decided to have the class collaboratively write a narrative poem, outlining the plot of the novel. We reviewed narrative poetry and chose an AABB rhyme scheme, and each student selected a chapter for which to write a quatrain or two. We didn't choose a communal meter, that being a little too challenging and time consuming for this activity, but I mentioned that all poets would want to be consistent within their own stanzas. Students were permitted either to choose one chapter and work alone or work in pairs on two consecutive chapters. There were 22 students, and since the novel has 23 chapters, I was left with a chapter to model on the board. Since I hadn't planned doing this in advance, the class was able to observe my drafting process. I pointed out that their classmates would receive copies of the poem and would use it, along with their reading journal entries, to locate information in the book for their essays; therefore, the poets needed to include as much information in their stanzas as possible.

It was probably not by chance that I was left with the sensitive chapter of preteen Jonas's awakening feelings, but as we had read, the Community takes care of that immediately, as I reveal in my stanza:

> After seeing Fiona, Jonas had a dream;
>
> They were about feelings that weren't what they might seem.
>
> Mother said, "Stirrings are what these feelings we call.
>
> At 12, the Community takes pills to stop them all.

I point out that everything I underlined is a fact from the chapter.

By the end of the period, the class had created a narrative poem of the entire book; some stanzas were better and more accurate than others. For a classwork grade, I assessed the stanzas on the basis of accuracy and amount of information from the story.

Brittany and Amanda wrote about one of the chapters where the reader hears of Release:

> Volunteering at the House of Old—
>
> This community was really controlled.
>
> Talking about the Olds' Release,
>
> Sent Elsewhere at their age increased.

Anthony's Chapter 11 depicts Jonas's first day as Receiver of Memories:

> It was Jonas's first day, and he did something weird,
>
> When he was touched on the back with a man with a beard.
>
> He appeared on a hill with some snow and a sled,
>
> Even though he was really lying on top of a bed.

And Karim's Chapter 23 shares the ambiguous ending:

> Gabe was cold and weak, and Jonas was sad,
>
> But when they reached the hill, it was not bad.

> Going down the hill, Jonas saw red, blue, and white.
>
> He and Gabe heard music from a very far height . . .

When the poem was completed, a student typed it and distributed copies for us to read together. Because students knew that their classmates would be reading each stanza and were relying on each other for a review prior to the concluding writing assignment, no one let us down—the gap would have been obvious. The result of the activity was a successful poem, as well as an effective and efficient review. In this case, the reformulation functioned as a review, a collaborative writing activity, and a useful tool for future assignments.

## THE POST-READING EVALUATIVE RESPONSE

On Bloom's taxonomy (1956), the most complex cognitive level is evaluation or making judgments as to the value or purpose of something. During the year, I teach my students to evaluate the books they are reading but also slowly to build from simple evaluative responses to book reviews and book talks to, in some advanced cases, literary critiques.

At the beginning of the year, after I introduce and teach journaling and the students start writing a five-minute anticipation or preview responses and daily during-reading responses, I tell them that on the day they finish their books, they are to write a more general response, a response to the book *as a whole* (see "Starting and Finishing a Book" guidelines in Chapter 3). We discuss what would go into the general response, such as the resolution of the conflict or how the denouement or epilogue, if any, enhanced the book; an overall look at the plot; and whether they liked the book and why and possibly even how they felt about finishing it. This is not the time to introduce the nuances of evaluation but to create a short response to the whole book. We practice by reading a three- or four-page story where we stop and write responses to the first and second pages and then write a response after the last page that may focus on the last part but also addresses the entire story. This is a five-minute response, and I am building a scaffold for more in-depth evaluation later in the year.

Ceire finished reading *After the Rain* by Norma Fox Mazer:

> I must say that I really enjoyed this book. It was slow moving in the beginning, but it did not take long to pick up. I love how the author made Izzy a mysterious character. By this, I mean that you had to keep reading to understand him. The way he acted and how he talked reminded me of my Poppop. Rachel's and Helena's friendship was fun to read about because they seemed to be polar opposites, yet they got along so well. The story of how they became friends was quite amusing, if I do say so myself. The best part, well, parts of the book were when Rachel and Lewis were together. Lewis is so funny and the voices he makes I almost hear when I read them. He was there for Rachel when things went really bad which is good because if he left I would have had to put down the book out of anger. Overall this was a good book, and I would recommend it to friends and family.

I have an eBoard, which is somewhat like a simple website. I wanted a protected chat room where my students could share their books, ask questions of each other, and respond. I found that I was able to do this as a "note" on the eBoard. Initially I named this our "Book Blogs." Students are invited to write short reviews of their books. Usually they do so after they have finished a book, but some write while they are in the midst of a novel. I post the following directions:

1. Enter the title, author, and genre of a book you are reading and write a short review of the book to share with prospective readers. Make sure you support your opinions with reasons and your comments with examples.

2. You may respond or add to someone's review or comments or answer any questions they may ask about the book you reviewed.

3. You must sign your name to any comments.

A few students add to the blog each week. I offer them 5 extra points on their weekly journals to entice them to take the time to share. Those who post are generally quite enthusiastic about their books, as in these examples:

Lindsay: September 30, 2008

I have finished *The Diamond of Darkhold* by Jeanne DuPrau. If you have read the previous City of Ember books, this makes a REALLY good last book (so I think). Actually, I was just getting a book for my cousin's birthday when my mom saw the *Diamond of Darkhold*. She knew that I read the previous books. I thought that was kind of cool by the way. Anyway, *The Diamond of Darkhold* is about a village (Sparks) that is going through a struggle after the Disaster. They have to provide what they have for 400 additional members from the underground city of Ember. Also, the Emberites know nothing about weather, climate, above ground hazards, and other things. I really liked this book, and if you like fantasy books about other worlds but it is still realistic, you would enjoy this book very much!

Anna: October 8, 2008

I have finished another great book! *Ana's Story* by Jenna Bush is about a girl, Ana, and her life living with HIV/AIDS. I would say this book is for mature readers because there are very serious parts that need to be taken seriously. Also this book is probably a better for girl readers because we can connect with the way the character feels about everything. This book also has facts and websites in the back of the book on HIV/AIDS. This book is real and I like what Jenna Bush says at the end of the story, "This book must end, but Ana's story is still being written—this time, by her." This is a quick read because you get so into it, time flies! (Also it has larger print!) I hope you enjoy this book!!!

Andrew: October 14, 2008

I have finished this great book called *Generation Dead*. This great book is about these dead kids coming from the grave and going to high school. It was a very interesting plot. I've never read anything quite like it before. There are three protagonists in the story. One is Phoebe, a quiet Goth girl who is caring and very curious about the living impaired kids (dead kids). The second is Adam who is a jock who slowly falls in love with Phoebe. The last is Pete. He is the enemy of the story. He hates the living impaired kids with a passion and wants to destroy them, but under all this anger is a confused teenager who is suffering major loss issues. This book is great for anyone! I loved it and I'm sure anyone else who reads it will too.

Later in the year, the questions and comments generally increase as more students, and even some of their other teachers, begin posting and students read some of the books that were recommended. The book blogs can serve as an introduction to the more comprehensive book reviews.

# BOOK REVIEWS AND BOOK TALKS

I have never spoken to students who saw the point of a book report beyond proving to the teacher that they read the book. When I introduce book reviews and book talks, I emphasize that the goal is to share the book with other readers who may want to read the book, whether or not the reader liked it. My primary objective is the sharing of books, although the book review also serves as an additional type of informational writing. Book talks permit me to teach, and students to practice, public speaking procedures and techniques.

## Book Reviews

First, I distribute three book reviews from a variety of sources to each student. I always include a page of student reviews from the National Council of Teachers of English's (NCTE's) *Voices from the Middle* because they are written by adolescent readers and, therefore, are less intimidating than "professional" reviews. I ask the students to read the sample reviews and, working in partners, make two lists. One list notes any type of information contained in all three reviews, such as title and author. The second list documents information that appears in some but not all of the reviews, such as price or number of pages. The first list becomes the "essential" elements in their reviews; the second list contains the "optional" elements. Together we make an official class list:

| Essential | Optional |
|---|---|
| Title | Number of pages |
| Author | Price |
| Publisher | Subplots |
| Copyright date | Comparison to other books |
| Genre | Awards |
| Short summary, including conflict | Reading level |
| Main characters (i.e., protagonist and antagonist) | Other books by author |
| Opinion | Illustrations |
| | Quotes from text |
| | Quotes from other reviewers |

We practice writing a review with our shared-reading novel so that we can compare results. Our practice review is to contain all essential information and four optional elements. I place a student review on the overhead, and we highlight the essential elements in one color and the optional elements in another. Students volunteer ways in which they included different information or wrote about similar facts in divergent ways. I share here Rachel, a former student's, independent novel review, an edited version of which was published in NCTE's *Voices from the Middle* "Student to Student" column:

> *Twilight*, written by Stephenie Meyer, ©2005; Little, Brown and Company; $8.99
> ISBN 0-316-1607-2 (hardcover) or 0-316-01584-9 (paperback)
>
> In this fantasy novel, Bella Swan is a 17-year-old girl who moves from the city of Phoenix to live with her father in the town of Forks, Washington. As she struggles to fit into a new school, she finds herself drawn to a classmate, Edward Cullen; he is unlike anyone she has ever met. Bella is taken aback when she learns that Edward is interested in her as well. There seems to be an undeniable attraction, like two magnets pulled together by a strong force. Bella comes to realize there is something mysterious about Edward, and he tries to warn Bella that he is dangerous and they should not be together. But they both cannot control their need to be with each other. Will their love survive?
>
> I recommend this highly romantic, yet suspenseful, novel. It is truly a book I could not put down. It pulled me in right from the beginning until the end. Just as the characters have this energy pulling them together, as a reader I felt driven to find out what happens to the characters. I could connect to the setting of the story, which takes place in a high school. Also, to the idea of being a new girl trying to fit in. Most importantly, I was intrigued by the idea of how people can feel drawn to another, very different, person.
>
> When you are finished reading, you'll still want to find out more about these characters and want to read the sequel, *New Moon*.

I inform the students that they will now be required to write one book review during each of the remaining marking periods; each review will contain all the essential information and at least three optional elements. I explain that we will include these reviews in the *Roessing Reader Reviews,* a three-ring binder that my students have added to for the last four to five years and that sits on one of our bookcases for reference. These reviews are categorized by genre, as is my class library, and students are encouraged to browse through them when looking for a book to read. I find that writers make more effort to write well, revise and edit their writings, and set up the pages effectively when they know others will be reading their reviews. This type of experience, publishing for a real audience, transforms students into authors. It also provides an authentic purpose for writing. In addition, I encourage students to prepare reviews for submission to *Voices from the Middle*'s "From Student to Student" column; Rachel's review was written in the format appropriate for submission and accepted for publication in the March 2008 issue. My students and I look for other places to publish throughout the year as well.

## Book Talks

The students lean forward. "Can you imagine *wanting* a vampire to bite you, begging him to do so? You, a typical, human, middle school or, in this case, high school student think you are in love for the first time. And your boyfriend is someone you have read about only in fantasy books . . ." As I finish, students storm my library. Luckily, I bought three copies of *Twilight*. Almost every time someone gives a book talk, at least one other student wants to read the book. The classroom buzzes after a good book talk with more book talk. Readers talk about whether they have read that book, another book by the same author, or similar books. They talk about whether they liked that book or the ones like it. They think about the books they are reading and make mental comparisons. The more book talk in the classroom, the more books read.

I start the year with a Book-Talk Hour, presented by a book talk expert, our librarian. We meet in the library where my students are surrounded with books, not only the books for the discussion but thousands of other books just waiting to be read. I tell my classes that they are going to the library to hear about books and that I want them to notice two things— the books the librarian introduces but also *how* she introduces them, what she includes in her very effective book talks. They note details like how she begins with a question, an anecdote, or a scene from the book. She connects the book to herself, to something in her life, to an interest she has or something she has wondered about, or even to them, her audience. In public speaking, that is called an "attention getter;" in writing, it is a "lead." They all notice that, for each selection, Linda gives the title, the author, the topic, the main characters, and some of the plot—just enough to get them interested but not enough to give it away. She may read an excerpt or talk about the authors and other books they have written. Most importantly, she advises what type of reader may like a particular book. Students discern that analysis of the books has preceded the book talks and that even though these talks are for the students, the librarian is primarily a reader responding to her reading.

Besides writing about books, it is important for a classroom to be alive with talk about books, and for this reason I encourage book talks. In the Starting to Finishing a Book guidelines, book talks are listed as an extra-credit option, but it is obvious by the requirements listed that even though it is a voluntary, extra-credit assignment, a book talk is not a spur-of-the-moment, fly-by-the-seat-of your-pants experience but rather a prepared response to literature. I sometimes substitute mandatory book talks for the quarterly book reviews to ensure that everyone participates in the experience. Teachers can hold Book-Talk Days where students sit in small groups and give book talks within their groups, a process much more comfortable for the shy students. Even in these small groups, readers address an authentic audience, an audience who is interested in the reviewers' response to their books.

## LITERARY CRITIQUES

Literary criticism differs from a review in the degree of analysis and evaluation and forces the readers to probe deeper in their responses. The most important aspect of teaching literary criticism is determining the criteria by which to evaluate the text. I begin with something students know and are accustomed to critiquing, such as a restaurant. I asked them to list their criteria for judging a restaurant.

They brainstorm:

Food

Service

Ambiance

Location

We further divide the categories:

Food—amount, variety, taste, cost

Service—friendliness, speed

Ambiance—cleanliness, comfort, decor, lighting

Location—distance from home, distance from shopping or entertainment

I group students by restaurants with which two or three are familiar, and each group rates their restaurant in three categories. Their challenge is to come up with the evaluative wording rather than "8 out of 10." Then we can progress to a topic closer to books—movies. Adolescents have lots of experience discussing movies with their friends and evaluating them. They tell me that they evaluate the acting, plotline, scenery or setting, special effects, music, cinematography, characterization, tone (e.g., if comedies are truly humorous and horror movies are really scary), and audience appropriateness.

With two examples under their belts, they are ready to critique their books. First we list elements readers can assess for value or effectiveness: plot, setting, characters, characterizations, writing style, tone, theme, length, readability, and audience appropriateness. I stress that each criticism needs to be supported with specific examples from the text. As readers write critiques, they delve more profoundly into their initial responses to the book. I only require literary critiques of students who are ready for critical thinking and then only after we have worked through other types of evaluative response.

## ADAPTATIONS

Text reformulations do not need any type of formal adaptations in instruction since students can choose their type of reformulation and, in many cases, will be working collaboratively. Teachers can choose the groups for whole-class shared readings to balance presentations. Teachers can also differentiate requirements for and frequency of book reviews and can group students for book talks. For less advanced readers, reviews typically take the place of critiques; in many schools, literary critique is not introduced until high school.

# PART IV

## Content Area Response Adaptations

# 10

# Responding Across the Curriculum

Over 75 percent of an adolescent's school day is spent in content area classes. In most subjects, much of class time involves reading—textbooks, articles, handouts, notes, or directions. Although most of the examples in this book are responses to literature—fiction and nonfiction—all the techniques discussed can be applied effectively to content area text.

The majority of reading both in and out of school is informational reading; therefore, it is crucial to teach this genre. My language arts classes study informational reading as a genre, and I include informational texts, when appropriate, to supplement and enrich any shared literary texts. Content area teachers need to guide their students' informational reading to help them better comprehend their textbooks.

## NONFICTION TEXTS

In my classes, I widely employ nonfiction texts. I teach strategies for reading nonfiction as a discrete genre, and I also use nonfiction texts to supplement literary units. Magazine, news, and Internet articles; letters; speeches; historical documents; and other primary and secondary sources provide background and enrichment for shared and small-group readings, whether of short stories, poems, or novels.

Understanding nonfiction is essential to academic achievement in all content areas. Whether teachers—of language arts or of a content area—teach nonfiction strategies independently or as part of a content unit, encouraging reader response increases student awareness of *what* they are reading through text interaction and allows teachers to discern *how* and *if* their students are making meaning from the content. Expository reading requires knowledge of additional text structures and familiarity with nonfiction features and elements, such as tables of contents, indexes, and glossaries; headings and subheadings; footnotes and citations; maps, charts, timelines, and graphs; graphics and typefaces; as well as the content being read and learned. Teachers can prepare focus lessons for any of these structures or features and ask students to look at text—either handouts or textbooks—and respond. In this lesson, nonfiction elements are the focus, just as literary elements are the focus of lessons on fiction, and the reading strategies are the same.

## TEXT FEATURES

Informational texts—textbooks, magazines, newspapers, and other nonfiction writings—look different from fiction texts. The authors or editors include distinctive elements, generally identified as "text features," that support student reading of and learning from those texts. I tend to refer to these tools as "text assistants," because they assist in such reading comprehension strategies as activating prior knowledge, purpose setting, predicting, visualizing, and making connections (especially connections between texts or texts and other learning). Text features are most apparent in student textbooks, although they may appear in general-interest magazine and news articles as well as informational books. Student textbook reading becomes more proficient if content area teachers teach the reading of informational text in their content areas, emphasizing the use of text features. In doing so, they can focus on their particular textbooks and any supplementary materials used in the class. It is essential that readers become skilled in using these aids and become cognizant of how text features increase comprehension of a topic.

The most common text features are the following:

- Tables of contents
- Headings and subheadings
- Photos and illustrations and captions
- Maps and map keys
- Charts
- Graphs
- Diagrams
- Timelines
- Glossaries
- Indexes
- Information boxes
- Bullets
- Bold or italicized text
- Font type and size

For example, after explaining or reviewing text features and their purpose in facilitating better comprehension of informational texts, I have had the class discuss their textbooks for other classes as well as the articles we had read in conjunction with our most recent literary unit. For one guided practice, I distributed an article on wolves and asked the students to read it, highlighting any text features they noticed. Next they identified those features in the margins, and when they finished reading, each wrote a five-minute response, reflecting on the information in the article and the text features specifically. We listed the text features noted and discussed how they facilitated comprehension of the text.

The article discussed the endangerment of wolves. One solution presented was reintroducing wolves to certain states in which wolf populations were diminished. The students agreed that even though the states were named in the text, it was much easier to comprehend the effects of the distribution by looking at the map that highlighted existing wolf populations in one color and the states in which wolves were being reintroduced in another color. Readers could easily perceive how the distribution was spread throughout the country. Anthony pointed out,

> I am familiar with those states, but when they are only mentioned by name in the text, I cannot readily picture their locations, especially in respect to each other and the country as a whole. The map made the author's point clear.

Many other students agreed. By reflecting on the text feature, Anthony was able to examine how he used this feature and how it aided comprehension and, consequently, take charge of his own learning. To take metacognition one step further, if a future text did not include such a tool, Anthony might think to look up a map and plot the distribution, increasing his comprehension of the text.

The students were to read informational texts of their choice as their independent reading, and the utilization of text features was our focus lesson. I posted my reading response assignment for that week (see Figure 10.1).

**Figure 10.1**  Sample: Response to Informational Text

This Week's Independent Reading—Informational Text
Books, Magazines, or Newspapers

This week you are to read information texts of your choice.

I. If you are reading an entire informational book, enter the book on your "Record of Books Read."

II. As usual, for either books or magazines or newspaper articles, enter the following on your Daily Log:

1. The title of the article or section of a book and the title and date of the newspaper, magazine, or book

2. The amount of time and pages read

III. Read for 25 minutes/night and respond for 5 minutes, reflecting on the information read and . . .

IV. The Focus Lesson for this week:

1. Note any informational text features that are different from those of narrative text, such as a table of contents, italicized words, section headings and subheadings, graphics and (more importantly) . . .

2. *How* any text features helped you comprehend better.

Taylor read *Girls Who Rocked the World* and reflected,

> In my book, there are subtitles and also information boxes. The subtitles have the famous person's job or why they are important and their birth and death dates. For me, that is helpful. I would choose to read if any girl's job or the name caught my attention. When I read, I usually become distracted by the information boxes. I am still glad they are there because usually the most interesting facts are there. Also, I used the table of contents. This helped me to choose a girl who caught my interest rather than someone I didn't want to read about. When I read about

Queen Victoria I learned she was only aware of the throne when she turned 10. Just by reading the information box, I learned her father passed away. I found this [informational text] was different from fiction because I can skip around. I don't have to read right through.

Kelly focused on the value of the table of contents, index, and italicized words:

One text feature I noticed when reading this book was there was a table of contents. I found this helpful because I could skip around to different animals and learn about them without having to read the entire book. Another thing I found helpful was the italicized words. This meant that the words were important, so I took notice of them easier than the nonitalicized words. The index in the back was helpful because I could look up keywords and easily find them in the book.

Once students become familiar with nonfiction components, responding to the text is similar to response to any literary text.

## MARGINAL NOTES

As my first step in teaching nonfiction response, I distribute articles to the students. We discuss what goes through our minds as we read:

This is something new or foreign.

I agree; I disagree.

I already knew that.

What a new (innovative) idea! or I never knew (thought of) that!

This is a surprising (shocking) fact. or This idea is confusing.

I have a question.

I would like more information.

Then the class creates logos to label these responses within the text. I caution them to fashion simple, easy-to-draw symbols. The logos often look something like this:

☺ I agree.

☹ I disagree.

✗ New idea; I didn't know (think) this.

▤ I already knew (learned) this.

! Surprising idea (fact)

!! Shocking idea (fact)

? Confusing idea; I have a question.

⚲ I need (would like) more information.

✎ Future writing idea or ▱ future reading topic

At first, I introduce a reduced list until the students become more accustomed to reading and responding to nonfiction and to the logos. I do not want the students to spend more time looking at the symbols than reading.

I demonstrate using a short, high-interest article (newspaper articles work well for this), and the students work on guided practice. The content area teacher could use any news, magazine, or Internet article that complements the curriculum or a photocopied section of the textbook for this purpose. Students read the text, drawing their thought-logos in the margin. The marked-up articles are then ready for discussion. The teacher could ask students to discuss their general comments or focus on their questions. Alternatively, the teacher could group students by comments: one group to discuss questions, one to discuss new ideas, and so forth.

Marginal responses generate more conversation than directions to "read the article and discuss." They also lead to deeper reflection when students compare their responses. A natural extension of this task is to require students to choose three or four comments and respond further to them. Of course, students cannot mark in textbooks, but large sticky notes can be cut into one-inch strips, and students can temporarily attach them to the textbook margin.

A more advanced response activity is for learners to attach the marked-up strip in their response journals and further annotate. The same procedures can be used for nonfiction reading strategies, such as asking questions (?), noting important details (!), making connections ($\leftrightarrow$), inferences or predictions ($\uparrow$), or visualizations ($\circledcirc$).

## ELECTRONIC MEDIA—WEB SITE RESPONSE

Today is the age of instant information; our students travel on the Internet highway. Frankly, many school libraries cannot maintain resources that are as current as the Internet. People of all ages go to Web sites for information, whether for research, enrichment, background knowledge, or general interest. Reading instruction needs to integrate electronic media to prepare students for 21st-century literacies. Therefore, I make sure to explain search engines, conduct "Web talks" using a book talk format, and coach students to evaluate Web sites and respond to the information they find on them. In fact, response prepares students to *use* Web information rather than simply to copy it.

I teach the Web as a literary genre. Reading Web sites for information raises issues of validity and reliability. Students are aware that anyone can publish a Web site and that information on some sites can be revised by anybody. We discuss the expectations of different types of sites—.com, .org, .edu, and .gov—and methods to evaluate a site.

I then let my students practice responding to electronic media to ascertain their strategies and thinking. We discuss what they are studying in their classes. In our class, we were reading Daniel Keyes's short story "Flowers for Algernon" and learning about intelligence, IQ, and brain studies. In social studies, the students were studying the Underground Railroad and women's rights, and in science they were learning about nuclear fission. As a response assignment, I explained that I wanted them to choose a topic from one of their classes or an interest from their extracurricular life about which they wanted to learn more. We also brainstormed search engines and Web sites.

The assignment for their next Reading Journal was given as follows:

You are to reflect on and write a response to electronic media (an Internet Web site).

Choose a topic you are interested in, especially one that is connected to something you are studying in one of your classes (such as IQ and creativity or intelligence and personality) or a sport or activity in which you are involved, locate a Web site on that topic, and read the information.

1. In your journal reflect on the following:

   a) Why you chose that topic

   b) How you found/reached that particular Web site—the journey you took starting with the keyword(s) you used and/or tried

2. Evaluate the Web site.

3. Write a short response to your reading of the information on Web site.

Anthony shared his response to an article he found on a Web site (www.intelligencetest .com/articles/article4.htm).

### Process of Choosing Article

To start, I searched "IQ Articles" in Google. I then chose the first result. I explored it and found that it did not have what I was looking for. I went back to the search result page and chose the second result. There were a number of topics on this site, so I scrolled down to see that if there were any that interested me. As it turns out, there was one that suited me perfectly. The title was: "HIGHER INTELLIGENCE THROUGH MUSIC." Since I have a passion for music and also play three instruments, I selected it.

### Response to Article

As I read, I found something interesting that didn't surprise me. The article said that listening to Classical music helps you study and learn better. This makes sense to me because in my opinion, Classical music is soothing and peaceful. Now, something else was really cool. A group of researchers followed the progress of three year olds that were split into two groups. One group had no musical experience or exposure. The musical group, however, sang daily in chorus and studied the piano. After eight months, the musical kids were much better at solving puzzles. Also, when tested, they also scored 80% higher on spatial intelligence tests than the non-musical group. This must be true with me because I get straight A's and am very involved in music. It also stated that Stephen King, one of the greatest writers of our time, writes with loud rock music playing, just look at well he is doing. So, I guess it depends on the uniqueness of our brain; which relates back to our discussion in class about how brains function differently for every one of us.

### Evaluation of the Article

This web site was great. You did not need a PhD to comprehend the information. Also, the article was written by someone who studies brains and their activity for a living. Overall, I know that my music is helping me with my studies, which is good, because I plan to continue music through my adult career. This article helped confirm that.

Taylor's Web quest was more personal:

Sleep/Dream Patterns

Website: www.rationality.net/sleepdreams.htm

I chose the topic sleep and dream patterns because my brother has sleep apnea. This will help me understand what goes on while he sleeps. I found my research by starting with the word "dream." I found that my results were too broad. Then I used "sleep" and again the same results. In the end I searched "sleep and dream patterns" and my research topics were narrowed down. I also looked at quotes and the research the website used. All were books by professors. I have actually learned a lot about sleeping and dreaming. Your dreams are based on your mood and life experiences. Most importantly, you should remember not to allow your dreams to affect your decisions. We sleep to keep our body healthy and so we can function. Finally, most theories are made by observing animal sleep. A question I will end with is will all animals' sleep patterns be exactly like ours. All in all, everyone's sleep and dreams are different.

Carlin's response was based on the independent novel she was reading, *Scribbler of Dreams*. She remembered that I had introduced it in a book talk as a "modern-day *Romeo and Juliet*." As a motivated reader, she wanted to become familiar with the plot of *Romeo and Juliet* because she thought that would help her comprehend and enjoy her novel more. I suggested that she find an online plot summary. Her journal entry shows that she not only read the summary but that she connected it to her reading, which also led to inferences and predictions.

I choose this topic [Romeo and Juliet] because I am reading Scribbler of Dreams, which is a present-day book with the same story as Romeo and Juliet. I wanted to know more about Romeo and Juliet because I thought I would appreciate Scribbler of Dreams more than I do now.

I went under Yahoo and I typed in 'Romeo and Juliet' There were a lot of searches on the movie, but no synopsis. So I scrolled to the top and I saw a link that said 'Synopsis on Romeo and Juliet.' So I clicked that and I picked the first one because the other ones were Wikipedia links.

I liked the web site. The synopsis was really long, and I skimmed through most of it, but when it came to the real story part, closer to the end, I thought I learned a lot about Romeo and Juliet, and I definitely appreciated Scribbler of Dreams more. Reading the synopsis made me think that Scribbler of Dreams would end like Romeo and Juliet, so I wasn't going to read it. But then I thought that it would be weird if a story in present day had Kait poisoning herself and then Bram killing himself. I was happy I went back and read it because it was completely different than Romeo and Juliet, and I wasn't predicting any killing in the end.

> Romeo and Juliet and Scribbler of Dreams are basically the same story because in both books, there is a romance between two lovers, which becomes hard for them when the other's family is the enemy to the others. They both have to hide their identities and lie about who they truly are. Bram is a Hampton, and Kait is a Malone. Both the Hampton and Malone families hate each other because Kait's father accidentally killed Bram's father. But when Kait falls in love with Bram, she can't tell him that she is Kait Malone because Bram's family hates the Malones. So she tells him that her name is Kait Hampton, so his family would like her.
>
> Some things that were different in the literary works would be that at the end of Romeo and Juliet, Juliet takes this poison that puts her in a deep sleep. When Romeo sees her lying there, he kills himself because he believes she was dead. But, when Juliet wakes up from her deep sleep, she kills herself because she sees him lying there dead. At the end of Scribbler of Dreams, Kait and Bram get in a fight when Bram finds out she is a Malone. They end up not talking for a couple weeks, but then end up back together after Bram finds the necklace he gave her on the ground. He gives it back to Kait, and they get back together.

It is essential to repeat and expand assignments to develop what students know or have already experienced. Each time, they improve and become more thoughtful about what they have accomplished, and the extension to the assignment challenges those who had success previously while giving a modification to those who still need more experience. Sometimes the subsequent assignment speaks to them more than the original Web site response. Other than Carlin and a few others, I did not feel that the students were making the connection between the Web information and the lesson(s) from which they chose their topic. A few weeks later, I modified and repeated the assignment.

During our study of the Holocaust and Anne Frank, I asked the students again to read and respond to an article on electronic media. I again gave an assignment:

> This week's focus lesson is enrichment information, a variant of activating prior knowledge. In class, we will read/act the play *The Diary of Anne Frank*; therefore, we will first learn background information about the Holocaust. This is a very complicated time period. For your nightly reading, you are currently each reading a book, fiction or nonfiction, set during the Holocaust.
>
> As one of your five responses for this week's Reading Journal, you are to find out more information about a topic mentioned in your book. While you are reading, identify a topic that you . . .
>
> 1. find interesting and wish to learn more;
>
> 2. find confusing and need to learn more; or
>
> 3. need to learn more about to comprehend or enrich your reading.
>
> Then search for a Web site on that topic, read the information, and in your journal reflect on why you chose that topic and how you found/researched that particular Web site—the journey you took, beginning with the keywords you tried.

Lastly,

    a. evaluate the effectiveness of the Web site;

    b. write a five-minute response to your reading of the information on Web site; and

    c. include how reading the information enhanced your reading and comprehension.

Alayna wanted to know more about Adolph Hitler's childhood, hoping it would help her understand him and our Holocaust study a bit better. She settled on a ThinkQuest Web site and wrote in her Journal:

The topic I chose was Hitler's childhood because I was interested and wanted to learn more about it. The keywords I used were "Hitler's Childhood."

I chose the website library.thinkquest.org/J0112264/Hitler1.html. This website looks like it has many facts about Hitler's childhood. The ThinkQuest Library web sites were created by students around the world who have participated in ThinkQuest competitions.

Hitler was the only survivor out of all his siblings, and his parents died when Hitler was very young. I'm sure this made the rest of his life miserable since he was considered an orphan. Something that surprised me was that Hitler's dream was to become a priest. He was also an artist but didn't do well in art school. The doctor who treated his mother's breast cancer was Jewish, so maybe Hitler thought he caused his mother to die. It also surprised me that two of Hitler's closest friends were Jewish. What doesn't surprise me, though, is that it says his father used to beat him.

This helps me to understand Hitler's motives better and clears up some of the questions I had about him.

Anna made a more direct connection to the book she was reading. She began her entry with her purpose for obtaining supplementary information:

In my book [*Memories of Anne Frank* by Alison Leslie Gold] they discuss the laws towards Jews. I found this interesting and wanted to learn more. I went to Google and used the keywords "Jewish laws during the Holocaust." The link I chose was called "Nazi Anti-Jewish Laws—Children of the Holocaust Discussion Guide." from adl.org [Anti-Defamation League].

After reflecting on some of the laws pertinent to her reading and inferring that these laws, issued 1933–1938, were still "active" during the period of her book, Anna concludes her response, her goal achieved: "I am glad that I found this site because it makes me understand the situation of the characters in my story. The difficulty they must have had living such a strict life, unable to be children. It is horrible."

During the remainder of the year, whenever students want or need supplementary information, they now would have the tools and experience to use electronic media. Additionally, they would be proficient in reflecting on what they learned and how this information related to their studies and their lives.

# CONTENT AREA READING

Many content area teachers say they do not feel comfortable "teaching" reading strategies, yet all teachers talk about purpose for reading, activating existing knowledge, noticing the important details, asking questions, summarizing, and making connections within the content area or to other content areas. Content area teachers may not talk specifically about "making inferences," but they do expect students to do so. In other words, employing reader response does not require one to be a reading teacher. Content area is read, and responding increases comprehension of the content.

# PRE-READING RESPONSE

Teachers recognize the power of having a purpose for reading. An anticipation response for a content area chapter will look different from one for a novel, but teachers can ask students to look at text features—chapter or article titles, structures, headings and subheadings, pictures, charts, graphs, boldfaced or italicized words—and consider the previous unit of study, if applicable, to write an anticipatory response. Pre-reading response provides students with a purpose for reading and activates any knowledge they might already have. An alternate response is a prior-knowledge response. The teacher writes the topic on the board—World War I, fractions, global warming—and the students respond in either freewrite or list format.

Lilya, Mike, and Kevin browsed the chapter in their social studies textbook on the Cold War. They were asked to look at the title and subtitles, pictures, drawings, charts, and any terms that were bolded or in italics. Lilya wrote an anticipation response in which she focused on a few details, such as the chapter title, a political cartoon, and a highlighted term, all from the beginning of the chapter. She began,

> The picture with the red octopus with an angry-looking face and the word "Communism" makes me think that maybe Communists had something to do with the Cold War. Either that or they wanted to rule the earth. The word "bipolar" is in bold, maybe because the war itself was bipolar, the two sides were too opposite and couldn't find common ground.

Mike's comments also showed his thought processes as he surveyed the chapter from beginning to end. It is apparent that he primarily obtained his information from the pictures and captions; he began with an overview of the period:

> Overall this is a subject I am highly interested in, after looking at the chapter. So much was going on all around the world, from good to bad. . . . There was the North America Treaty created. There was a leader named Fidel Castro taking over Cuba and turning it Communist. . . . One of the last major events that ended the Cold War was the tearing down of the Berlin Wall.

Kevin interpreted individual features that caught his attention:

> The use of the color red [in the drawings] reminds me of a concept called the "red scare." When I see the subtitle "A Bipolar World," I can't help but think of the mental condition. The cartoon on page 44 is interesting because it portrays Russia and the U.S. as equally evil.

Even though these thoughts are not connected at this point, Kevin has a scaffold on which to build his knowledge of this time period.

From their responses, it appears that all three students have set purposes for reading—to see if their inferences are correct and to build upon those ideas as they learn about this period in history.

# DURING-READING RESPONSE

## Journaling

Teachers can employ response journals in classes across the curriculum. Response journals can be folders with center prongs, such as those I use, or spiral notebooks, if most reading will be accomplished in school; alternatively, students can designate a response section within their subject binders. In every subject, teachers need to provide models and guided practices of response to content area articles. Teachers can distribute Response Starters or work with their classes to create appropriate Response Starters. These will vary, depending on the content areas.

Sometimes content area teachers pair their lessons with literary works. Katie's social studies class was studying the Civil War. In conjunction, students read a historical fiction novel, *Steal Away Home* by Lois Ruby. Katie responded in her journal,

> I hate how they used things called "hush puppies" to kill the bloodhounds. I understand that they did it so they didn't get killed, but I hate hearing about the death of any animal. I think that they were very smart to jump in the river. I like Jeep because he seems very smart. I think it is amazing how Jeep knows that Miz Lizbet Charles died from typhoid fever.

In this case Katie responded in her language arts response journal; I told that class they could use their social studies novel for their independent reading during those few weeks. If the social studies teacher used response journals, she might have asked the students to focus on information about the period of the Civil War and the war itself. However, one can see that Katie *is* learning about the time period by her references to "hush puppies" and "typhoid fever." She also illustrates that she understands the laws of the period:

> I was so scared when Marshall Fain came back and almost found out that Lizbet was staying there. If he had found out, everyone would have gone to jail for hiding a fugitive slave.

In another response, Katie comments on gender roles at the time:

> I thought it was cute that Pa said how, when he married Ma, she swore to love and honor, but not to obey him. I think she was brave to do that because, back then, men were seen as superior to women.

## Double-Entry Journals

Possibly the most adaptable and useful form for content area response is the double-entry journal. Through a double-entry journal, students can reflect on their thinking and responses to new material in any content area. Using a simple, two-column journal labeled "From the TEXT—From Your BRAIN" (see Resource B, #18) is effective. Student-generated responses to the *National Geographic Kids News* article on the Ancient Olympics, referenced in Chapter 4, included the following:

> "Olympic truce"—In 1936, during the Holocaust, the Olympics were held in Germany. Obviously some type of truce had to be called, or at least Hitler hid what was going on.

> "Greeks thought Zeus was the leader of the many gods and goddesses they believed in."—So it was a *real* religion, not just the myths that we read!

A few social studies students who read the textbook chapter on the Cold War, the chapter for which Lilya, Mike, and Kevin wrote the anticipation responses, were asked to respond using the double-entry format. Jimmy responded to the United Nations' mission "to preserve world peace by promoting international cooperation," reflecting, "How hypocritical nations are when they are in it [the United Nations], attacking others on something they do themselves." When he read that "the United States sent vast amounts of money to 16 European nations," he responded,

> This was a plot of a <u>Simpsons</u> episode where the U.S. plans to send a trillion dollar bill under this plan, but it's stolen. I could tell the writers of the episode were against it because of the jokes they made about Europe.

It seems that Jimmy had been learning about historical events before he knew just where, when, and how they fit in, and his response let him activate the knowledge and reflect on the connection.

Courtney made a connection between information from the Holocaust study she had completed in language arts to the Cold War chapter. She noted that "millions were imprisoned in labor camps. Instead of a worker's paradise, the Soviet Union became a brutal dictatorship," and responded: "This reminds me of the Holocaust. Tons of people were imprisoned; they were forced to do work until they died sometimes, and the Nazis seemed like they were heavily disciplined too."

John, reflecting on the fact "these 'superpowers' were the United States and the Soviet Union," analyzed the situation: "There is bound to be tension between these two nations. If there are two superior countries, then they will both strive to be the best. The world is power hungry, and there cannot be two number ones."

John's double-entry response journal includes a connection made to a literary work read in our language arts class earlier in the year, *Haroun and the Sea of Stories*, and demonstrates a true "responding across the curriculum" (see Figure 10.2).

It is remarkable that the four students chose different sections of the chapter for their responses. The resulting journal responses generate interesting class discussions and ensure that discussions continue after the initial reading of the chapter. When teachers give discussion questions, students only note what they are asked to notice, and discussions, more frequently, are one-dimensional.

A colleague employed double-entry responses with her fifth-grade science class using the material in Chapter 4 and copies of the content area double-entry form. Carol read an article on dolphins with her students and modeled a few double-entry journal responses. From the text, she wrote in her left-hand column, "Dolphins look alike." In the right-hand column, she queried, "How do dolphins recognize each other?" As the class continued to read the article, her students wrote their journal responses.

These first responses were predominantly questions. For example, reacting to the idea that "Dolphins swim in groups," Jenna has lots of questions: "Can dolphins swim when

| Figure 10.2 | John's "Cold War" Double-Entry Journal |

**Double-Entry Response Journal**

Subject <u>Cold War</u> Chapter <u>30</u>     Pages <u>435</u> to <u>449</u>

| From the TEXT (facts, quotes) | From your BRAIN (thoughts, reactions, opinions) | Page |
|---|---|---|
| 1. The Un was founded to preserve world peace by promoting international peace. | With a union this large wouldn't world domination always be on their mind? Although it is meant to promote piece I could see this turn into another war and the UN dominating the entire war. | 435 Question |
| 2. These "superpowers" were the United States and the Soviet Union | There is bound to be tension between these two nations. If there are two superior countries then they will both stride to be the best. The world is power hungry and there cannot be two number ones. | 436 prediction |
| 3. They saw the communism as a cruel system that took away peopl's... freedom of speech. | This goverment, communism, reminds me of the Chup's way of ruling in the novel Haroun and the Sea of Stories. In both, the citizens are unable to have free speech. The United States feels this to be wrong the way the Gupees felt the Chup's to be wrong. | 437 text to text |
| 4. During the cold war, the United States, and the Soviet Union rushed to build nuclear weapons. | This amount of nuclear weapons being made must have really required a lot of workers and provided a lot of jobs. What happend to these workers after the threat was over. I guess they were layed off. How did they dispose of these nuclear weapons? It must have been really dangerous. | 441 Question |

they were just born? Do they get better at swimming as they grow up? What do they call their groups?" Michael wanted to know, "Do they help each other if one got hurt?" Vishal inquired, "Do they get along always in groups?" and "Can dolphins leave their own groups?" On the other hand, Jeremy inferred a reason for the group swim: "They swim in groups so they can protect each other from predators."

Many students were intrigued with the fact that "dolphins babysit." Deana inquired, "How old do dolphins have to be before they can babysit?" and, on the flip side, "How old before dolphins don't have to be babysat?" Michael asked a practical question, "What do they get paid—shrimp?" One can see that these young students not only reflected on what they learned but were curious to learn more.

Next the students read an article on the ecosystem and took notes. They used the double-entry journals to reflect further on their notes. Some of the children commented on a newly learned fact, "Prey are hunted, and predators do the hunting." In her journal,

Victoria asked an insightful question: "Could a predator be prey?" Ryan made a connection to something he already knew (answering Victoria's question), as he quoted from the song "The Old Lady Who Swallowed a Fly." He noted,

> Old Lady eats a fly and then she ate a spider to kill the fly and ate a bird to kill the spider and a cat to kill the bird and then a dog to kill the cat and a goat to kill the dog and a horse to kill the goat, and then she died.

Ryan then created a third column on this paper and asked a question: "Can all kinds of animals kill other animals?"

In contrast, Elle made two charts—one in the left column and one in the right (see Figure 10.3). Elle's chart demonstrated the extent of her understanding of the lesson and helped her teacher to monitor exactly how she interpreted the material presented and

**Figure 10.3** Elle's Ecosystem Double-Entry Journal

#___ Name Elle Date 2/6/08 Chapter____

Summary: The ecosystem is a community that has living creatures and food webs like a jungle.

| From **BOOK**: Character, Setting, Event, Quote | From **BRAIN**: Your personal response, inference, questions | Page |
|---|---|---|
| 1. Food Web<br>when a animal eats a smaller animal. | Shark → to big fish<br>big fish → to small fish<br>small fish → to plankton<br>plankton → to seeweed | |
| 2. A whole forest is an ecosystem because animals live in it, breath in it and is apart of it. | Is a log an ecosystem.<br>Do animals live in logs. | |
| 3. Biotic + Abiotic<br>↓ living / breathing / alive<br>↓ not living / not breathing / not alive | Biotic: dogs, bears, tiger, penguin, polar bears<br>Abiotic: rock, chips, card board | |

what inferences she made. Her chart shows excellent scientific reasoning, illustrating how this format can help students create hypotheses.

Using these journals, teachers can determine *how* and *if* their students are making meaning from the content. They can discern how to proceed with additional material and the need to differentiate subsequent lessons.

## Poetic Response

Poetic response is applicable to any content area reading. Poetry response might be the most valuable and/or interesting response mode, since it requires more creative thinking and integrates divergent types of thinking. Students can easily write a found poem based on a section or chapter of any textbook in any subject. To write a found poem, the student takes (or *finds*) significant words and phrases from the text and forms them into a poem, usually as free verse poetry (see Chapter 5). The words the readers use show what they find to be essential, and the manner in which they combine them demonstrates their thinking. In this application, teachers should encourage students to add conclusions drawn from the reading. After reading an article on wasps, "The Kind of Face Only a Wasp Could Trust" in *Discovery Magazine* (Netting, 2005), I modeled a found poem to which I added a conclusion:

Black Splotches

Denoting social status

Bringing less work,

Showing body strength

Revered—always.

Cheaters

Sign of weakness,

Bringing humiliation,

Causing harassment.

Caught—always.

Wasp or Human

It doesn't pay to lie.

Another form of poetry, poetry in two voices (see Chapter 5), guides students to compare and contrast, a valuable analytical skill in any content area. For example, creative social studies student-poets can write poems in two voices comparing historical figures with each other, with prominent social figures of today, or with the poets themselves. Many teachers have transient students who would identify with a pioneer child moving westward or a Native American child on the Trail of Tears. Depending on the curriculum, social studies subjects for two-voice poetry could be an ancient Greek and Roman or Roman patrician and plebeian, an early American Indian and a European American colonist, a Union soldier and a Confederate soldier, or even General Lee and General Grant. A budding scientist could compare chemical compounds (chemistry), earth and

Mars (astronomy), the earth today and the earth of eons ago or of the future (geology), a deer and a lion (ecology), or a mussel and a limpet (marine biology). In science or math class, students could write a poem in two voices for "The Metric System Versus the English System." An adapted form, poetry in multiple voices, could give voice (literally) to various geometric shapes, comparing and contrasting a square, triangle, and a hexagon.

Here is a simple model for a science class:

| *The Lion* | *The Deer* |
|---|---|
| | |
| **I am a mammal, wild.** | |
| | |
| Our males have manes; | |
| | |
| | Ours grow antlers. |
| | |
| I roam the plains, | |
| | |
| | I roam the forests, |
| | |
| **Seeking food and shelter. I travel in a group called a** | |
| | |
| Pride. | |
| | |
| | Herd. |
| | |
| I am a carnivore; I feast on animals. | |
| | |
| | An herbivore, I nibble on vegetation. |
| | |
| **I am** | |
| | |
| The predator. | |
| | |
| | The prey. |

Writing "I Am" poetry is a Zenlike experience as the writer becomes the subject of the poem. Social studies curricula provide a never-ending supply of characters, such as King Tut, an adolescent in ancient Rome, a traveler on the Oregon Trail, and Abraham Lincoln before or after the Civil War. Student models of "I Am" poems for Holocaust victims are included in Chapter 5. Entering math class, "I Am . . . π," pays tribute to the well-known mathematical constant, a number that has its own calculator key. In "I Am . . . a Hypotenuse," the writer can combine the "I Am" form and poetry in two voices as the Hypotenuse "character" describes the power of being the longest side while exploring the feelings of the other two triangle sides. Science class can pay homage to "I Am . . . a Volcano" (geology), "I Am . . . Climate Change" (ecology), or "I Am . . . a Drop of Water." I created a sample of a poem on this last topic as an example for science teachers:

I am . . . a drop of water.

I am made up of . . . hydrogen and oxygen.

I create . . . bodies of water, like lakes, seas, oceans.

I help . . . plants grow.

I am needed by . . . all life.

I am . . . water.

I am needed for . . . hydration.

I need . . . a moist environment made up of others like me.

I hate . . . the sun; it dries me up.

I evaporate, form clouds, and drop again as rain.

Meg wrote an "I Am" poem in response to what she learned about chestnut blight:

I am a Chestnut tree.

I covered the eastern forests.

I provided nuts to people and animals.

I created strong wood for homes and lumber.

I was stymied by blight almost a century ago.

I now cower below taller trees, unable to grow.

I produce no chestnuts, nor wood.

I have been replaced by hickory and oak.

I am barely remembered by the present generation.

I could one day return to prominence,

if only I could best this vicious disease!

I am a Chestnut tree, once proud and strong.

Narrative poems tell a story, complete with characters, setting, and plot. Social studies teachers can use many published poems, such as Longfellow's "The Midnight Ride of

Paul Revere," as a model. Then their students can write their own historical poetry, such as "The Writing of the Gettysburg Address," "The Building of the Pyramids," or "Roanoke." For science and math teachers, narrative poetry assignments may pose more of a challenge, but myths were written to explain natural phenomena; students can write modern versions that are more scientifically based, such as "The Story of a Rainbow." Narrative poems of math problems provide creative methods of practicing for state standardized tests, which ask students to explain the steps used in solving problems. In addition, the whole class or smaller groups of students could collaborate on a narrative poem as a chapter or unit review (see Chapter 9). As a model, "The Ballad of $H_2O$" provides a brief narrative poem for a chemical compound:

Two Hydrogens marry;

They have a daughter.

They name her Oxygen,

And together they make WATER.

## Note Passing

Collaborative learning affords multiple benefits. Group work provides instant feedback and a sense of audience, elements often missing from the classroom experience. Engaging with peers helps students understand that they learn as a part of a community. In addition, collaboration mirrors real-world work situations, as professionals often collaborate on presentations, reports, and projects.

For note passing, students read a problem and then respond on a note that is then passed around the members of their group; each student adds input or interpretation and reacts to the other group members' thoughts (see Chapter 6). Passing notes is an effective first step toward collaborative effort. Reading notes may help a student more fully understand and consider multiple interpretations of a problem or concept, resulting in true learning. This technique develops some students into teachers and others into debaters as they expound on their theories, which they have rehearsed on paper. If Susan doesn't understand a problem, Justin can explain his understanding or solution, and then Jessie can write about her interpretation or proposed solution. If Amanda understands, her interpretation on paper may lead Sean to think more critically about the problem before he writes that he "didn't get it." Since the note is being passed around, no one has to be "right" at the start. Learners are sharing what they think about the math problem, the science hypothesis, or the social studies concept without intimidation, arguing, or talking over or around each other. After considering all angles through note passing, the group is ready to collaborate on finding the solution or interpretation—the answer. At this point, they shift to discussion response.

## AFTER-READING RESPONSE

A chapter or a unit does not always need to conclude with a test or an essay. What is most important is ascertaining that students have learned and can apply the material. If not, the class can revisit the material and learn what they missed before continuing. Text reformulation (see Chapter 9) causes students to take information and manipulate it into another format, requiring them to return to the text. On the other hand, if students have learned content so thoroughly that they are able to synthesize it without support—our ultimate goal as teachers—reformulation allows students opportunities to develop and expand upon this new knowledge.

Some ideas for text reformulation in the content areas are an ABC list or book, a narrative review poem, or adaptations of any of the examples and suggestions explained in Chapter 9. Students responsible for different sections of a unit can collaborate on an after-reading response project, demonstrating how the various aspects of the topic interconnect.

## The Rationale

All these methods and techniques of response, used individually, collectively, and/or cumulatively, throughout the year and across the curriculum result in Rosenblatt's (2005b) "innumerable relationships between readers [or learners] and texts" (p. 17).

# PART V

## Response Evaluation

# 11

# Teacher and Student Evaluation

## FORMATIVE ASSESSMENT

How do teachers know *what* students are reading, *when* they are reading, *how much* they are reading, and, more importantly, *how* they are reading? The Daily Logs inform me when and how much my students are reading. I encourage readers to log in truthfully. I advise them that I realize it is unrealistic to think that they read exactly the required 25 minutes each night, that I assume on some days they will read a little less, and that I hope on some days they will become so engrossed in their books or have more time in school to read and will read more. I am not as concerned with the number of pages as with the time spent reading, although I hope to see their reading become more fluent during the year. I point out and demonstrate that some texts require a more deliberate reading, while others are easy to "breeze through"; some nights we all read more slowly than on others, and at some points in a book, our reading rate fluctuates. I advise my readers that it is important to keep an accurate record so that they can analyze their own reading habits.

### Assessment of Independent Reading

Response journals can serve as mini conferences with each student. As I read journal entries each week, I see what my students are reading and how they are reacting to the text, the storyline, and the characters. From my knowledge of many of the books they read and my experience with text structure, I can usually tell if they do not comprehend what they are reading. I can see if they are able to apply the focus lessons on reading strategies, text features, and literary devices that I have taught. I observe reading strategies employed when they draw what they visualize and note the words or phrases that led to these visualizations; when they connect the text to their lives and, as the year progresses, are able to identify the significance of these connections; or when they make predictions and cite the clues that led to those predictions. I can perceive when readers identify literary elements and devices we have studied and when they note elements of the writer's craft discussed in reading or writing lessons. I also notice when I need to reteach a concept, either individually, in a small group, or to an entire class. I hear the voices of the shy or hesitant students—the ones who are afraid to raise their hands in class discussions. As with any journal writing, I become conscious of what students sometimes *need* to tell me about their reading and their lives.

As authentic assessment of reading, I can provide "feedback, document progress, and make instructional decisions regarding that student—three of the primary reasons we grade" (Wormeli, 2006, p. 19).

Reading their journals, I also have the opportunity to respond individually. Each child has my attention as I read and individually monitor that student's thoughts. Sometimes I write a book recommendation or a note about when I read the same book or another book by the author; sometimes my response is a question or a congratulatory or encouraging phrase. At times, I have even suggested that students recommend their books to other students who also enjoy that genre or author, or I recommend that they confer with other students—in their class or in one of my other classes—who are reading the same books. Sometimes I can offer comprehension suggestions. When Da'Sha wrote that the Italian words in *Stones in the Water* confused her, I pointed out that some words were followed by an explanation of the word and other times the contiguous sentences provide clues. The novel remained challenging for her, but with those suggestions, she persevered and finished the book.

I know that my students are aware that I am reading their responses. Many times, almost unconsciously, they write personal comments to me in the midst of their responses. In December, Da'Sha wrote,

> I actually thought you were crazy when you said if I read 25 minutes a day for 5 days a week [it] will change my reading level. But you are not crazy because my parents and I can tell the difference between the beginning of the year to now.

I assumed that I was the crazy person she was addressing, and besides making me laugh and feel pleased that Da'Sha was perceiving an improvement in her reading, I realized that she took it for granted that I read every word she writes.

I also understand that my reading of their journals is important to students. One student wrote that she liked response journals because she felt like she was "sharing her books and her thoughts with another person." Many readers recommend their books and insist that I read them when they are finished. In this way, I have read some books I have really enjoyed, such as *The Five People You Meet in Heaven, Twilight,* and *Daughter of Venice.* I have come to know my students as readers. I bring in books that particular readers would like; they appreciate it and do the same for me. The reading journals and communication make me a part of the reading community, and I become a liaison among members of the community.

## The Assessment Process

I quickly learned to have each class turn in their journals on a different day of the week. Wanting to return Reading Journals the day they are submitted, I cannot claim that I always read every entry. I ask readers to put an asterisk next to the one entry they would like me to read in the event that I do not have the opportunity to read all entries, but I must admit, I become so nosy about their reading that I generally skim the entire week.

Since I have 20 to 30 journals to read each day, I have found the best procedure is to sit down for a good read before I leave school for the day. However, if I can't hand the journals back the next day, readers can continue responding on composition paper and insert their responses when I do return the journals; this was one reason for using the pocket folders with center prongs as Reading Journals. Even students who are absent from class can continue to respond.

For expediency, I give each student a plastic sticky flag to place, protruding, at the spot where I am to begin reading that week. They can also use a small sticky note. I first look at the Record of Books Read to see what book the student is currently reading, then glance at the Daily Log to see that the number of pages is not substantially decreasing and that they are reading about 25 minutes per night. The Log also lists any articles or short pieces that don't appear in the Record of Books Read. I then flip to the sticky flag and read the week's entries. Since all journals are set up in the same way, the process runs smoothly. If I find loose papers in the pockets or papers out of order, we take a few minutes for "housekeeping" at the beginning of class when I return the journals. That could also be accomplished the previous day prior to collecting the journals.

# EVALUATIVE ASSESSMENT: GRADING

If a weekly Reading Journal contains the required number of entries, customarily five per week, I place a sticker following the last entry, showing that the student has earned a grade of 100 percent. I am amazed that even eighth graders still (or again) like stickers. If a Journal includes fewer entries, if I feel that the responses are not "five-minute journalings," or if a focus lesson has not been integrated into one of the responses, I prorate the grade. For example, in a typical week, four acceptable entries earn a grade of 80 percent; five entries, none of which integrate the week's focus lesson(s), earn 92 percent (our lowest A); five entries that are not five-minute writings for that particular student earn 65 percent. In other words, a student earns maximum grade for expected effort and a minimum grade for minimum effort. The number of responses expected may fluctuate, depending on school holidays, and, therefore, the maximum score earned may change. The grading is flexible for diverse assignments but is consistent and predictable. Each student knows why a grade has been earned.

The journal grade counts as a quiz grade each week. This grade needs to be significant because I want my students to know that reading and responding are important and because reading and responding constitutes the majority of homework for my class. I also sought a grading system that rewards consistency. A variant would be to count each entry as a daily homework grade. Of course, individual teachers will develop their own grading systems.

## Assessment of Shared Reading

When we are reading a shared text, responses, especially the double-entry journal, make it easy for me to monitor each student's understanding of the reading. Every day, the readers fill out a double-entry sheet for each chapter (see Chapter 4). Usually readers are required to complete two to three responses for each chapter and generally have two chapters to read as homework. I can require less reading from struggling readers, or in a heterogeneous class where I want to maintain the pace, I can require fewer responses from struggling readers.

After we discuss the chapters in class and I collect homework, I read over the readers' responses (in this case daily). I can read the responses and write short comments in about 45 minutes (2 minutes per journal). Sometimes I read all the entries, sometimes I pick and choose, and sometimes I skim. But I can easily determine who understood the reading and the depth of the thinking or understanding: first, to what do they choose to respond, and secondly, how they respond. All questions? All predictions? A combination? Either—*what* or *how*—can lead to a lesson. This may seem like a lot of time, but it is more efficient than holding 25 individual conferences. Granted, with more students, I would probably read a response from each chapter instead of reading all responses, reading more only from students about whom I am concerned. I do find their ruminations enjoyable, however.

It is easy to see who comprehends. When we read *The Giver* by Lois Lowry, both Dawn and Tyler wrote about when the Previous Receiver of Memories told Jonas to call him "the Giver." Dawn wrote, "I think that the book is called The Giver because the old Receiver is giving Jonas the power of memory and since the Receiver is giving Jonas power to see memory, the book is called The Giver." Tyler, however, did not quite get the point: "Did he want Jonas to call him the Giver because he gave Jonas the job of Receiver of Memory?" I was able to jot a quick note on her response to steer her in the right direction.

Frequently, teachers wish that they had the time to teach one-on-one. This is such a chance. Maci ended one response with "What other memories is the Giver going to share?" I wrote back, "What memories do you think might be important for him to transmit to Jonas?" Maci need not actually write the answer in another journal entry; by the time she reads this and would answer, we would be four chapters ahead, and the book would have answered the question. What is important is that she takes a few minutes to read over my comment and think about it the next day when I return the journal entries.

If I see that many readers have the same misconceptions, I can expand the discussion the next day while that part of the story is still fresh in their minds. The students are not penalized for their misunderstandings, as they would be on a quiz, because they receive full credit for completing the response.

I can also see when students go beyond comprehension to application and analysis. Anthony reacted to "climate control" by pointing out, "We need climate control due to global warming. If we had it, many animals would not die. But I wonder how they [the community in *The Giver*] did it." I found it interesting that he found some advantages to Sameness.

After I scan and credit their responses, the students add these sheets to their Reading Journals as a continuing record of the novel. Later they can refer back to these pages, and these responses become a part of their yearlong reading and response portfolios.

## Rationale

When teachers give tests on reading, they discover two things—if the student read and if the student noticed and remembered what the teacher thought was important. When a student responds to the reading, the teacher finds out two things—if the student read and what the student noticed and thought important. This is true for shared texts, small-group readings, and individual reading. I can't say how many times I've seen students race into homeroom before school and ask other students, "What happened in last night's reading?" This was their sole preparation for a potential quiz or class discussion.

Even when responding to a shared text and a particular focus lesson, it would be unusual for any two students to respond to the same portions of text, events, characters, or writing craft or to respond in exactly the same way. Since each week, multiple responses are due, the probability diminishes. Therefore, personal response leads to personal responsibility; each student has to do his or her own work. Students know what they have to do to "get the grade," and since the criteria are consistent, parents understand them.

Reading Journal assessment allows teachers to grade students individually and differentiate the grading criteria. I can determine the percentage credit if a student, particularly a struggling reader, writes five responses but doesn't follow instructions based on a focus lesson, and I can give full credit to a student who was absent for the focus lesson. A "five-minute" response may look different for students of different abilities. Likewise, some students can be expected to read more pages in 25 minutes than others. I find that I can grade on intent since there are no "correct" or "incorrect" answers. Because the journals are so multifaceted, students do not read each other's entries and whine, "Why did he get a higher grade than I did?" In short, the journal as a basis of grading allows for individualized expectations and grading based upon those expectations.

# "WHAT'S IN IT FOR ME?" STUDENT METACOGNITION AND MUSINGS

Even though teachers need to assess how students comprehend, equally important is self-assessment. Multiple times during the year, I ask the students to look at their Reading Logs and observe how they are reading. They survey the amount of time read and the number of pages read. I ask them to be honest in their accounting because even though they are supposed to read 25 minutes per night, if they read less, or more, they need to record it accurately so that they can determine how effective their reading is and if they observe any improvement as the year progresses. I emphasize that the records are more for them than they are for me.

Three or four times a year, the readers analyze their Reading Journals to see how, how much, and what they are reading. Some are surprised at how slowly they are reading and look at the variables: genre, topic, difficulty of reading level, when and where they are reading, and what else is going on in their lives at the particular time. Some are surprised at how fast or how much they are reading or how their reading has altered.

## First Marking Period Self-Analysis

After the first eight weeks of the term, I asked my language arts students to compute how many pages they were reading per session and to reflect on this. Even at that early date, readers were able to analyze their reading and generate some profound reflections. Samantha wrote about *how* she reads:

> I have realized by calculating my pages-read average that I read parts with more difficult writing longer [slower] than I would for a book that makes perfect sense to me. If a book is hard for me, sometimes I will look at the word or phrase and try to figure it out myself, but sometimes I will look it up 'til I know what it means. If I find a book with too many of those words in it, I stop reading that book because it gets to the point where I can't understand the whole book.

Shawn reflected on *when* he reads:

> I usually read more during my nightly readings than I do when I get my reading done at TEP [Team Enrichment Period—a daily 35-minute study period]. I read less in [language arts] class. I noticed that from my nightly readings I tend to read more on Mondays, Tuesdays, and Wednesdays. I start to slip on Thursday, Friday, Saturday, and Sunday. I get deeper into a book on the Focus Lesson days.

John focused on the *amount* he reads:

> I have noticed a few things about my reading for this year. One thing is about my speed. I was reading very slowly at the beginning of the year, and now I'm reading an average of ten pages a night. There is still room for improvement.

Karim was surprised at his daily average:

> I am very surprised that I read a lot of pages in my book in one day, which is about 10 or 20 pages. Also I am very surprised about the time I read which is between 20–25 minutes. I was surprised about my reading average because of how many more pages I am reading in that time.

This is a preliminary self-analysis of their reading patterns. As the year continues, the scrutiny goes deeper as they start to examine *why* they are reading at particular, or varying, speeds or amounts and they begin analyzing their Journal writings.

## After a Semester of Response

This past year, I gave students a questionnaire at the end of January that directed them to "look through your Reading Journal and think back over the first semester of reading. Has anything changed since last year?" I then asked them to consider a few questions, including "How do you, or do you, think responding to your reading has helped you to become a better reader?" I requested that they read over some responses from September and some more recent responses before they replied. Roughly 97 percent of the replies were positive reactions, and most readers were specific about how response helped them become better readers:

Tara noticed that

> responding has helped me become a better reader in many ways. Before I just concentrated on the storyline. Now I think more about what happened. I also think about the author's style. I make connections and inferences. I understand all my reading better when I respond. Responding helps me think about what I read and reread. Rereading is not something I would normally do.

Philip wrote about the influence of response on his understanding:

> I am reading more because the responses are helping me think while I'm reading. When I am reading I actually think what the author's message is and what he wants me to learn. I am understanding what I read because I am writing my thoughts down on paper. This helps me get to know the characters better and what the main point of the story is.

Morgan pointed out how her response has changed:

> My responses from the beginning of the year to now are really different. Now, I think I analyze more. I don't just go by the words. I try to figure out what they really mean instead of just glancing over. Responding to my reading made me a better reader because I think more about it.

Tim looked through his responses and was reflective about how response has made him think more meaningfully about his reading:

> During the first semester I saw, as I progressed through my entries, that my responses reflected deeper into my reading and did not stay shallow. In my opinion, responding has helped me as a reader because, as I read, I have more thoughts, comments, connections, and questions than I did before. The first time I did a reading journal I never thought it would have helped me this much as it did. More and more, I began to understand much more of what I read and can scratch more than the surface of a book.

Cindy wrote:

> I understand more of what I read, and I enjoy the book more. The journal makes me think more about my reading than I used to. Before it was just an assignment, but now it's a habit. . . . Responding has helped me to look for hidden messages. . . . The responses have opened up my mind, in a way, and helped me to ask more questions and really make sense of what the author says.

David pointed out the influence of response on reading enjoyment:

> I notice that I am writing more in my responses now than I did at the beginning of the year. I believe this is because I understand what I am reading better . . . because over time I have written more and more responses and have learned to pay more attention to what I am reading. I am enjoying my reading more now because I am reading more fluently and it makes it a lot easier to understand what is happening in the book.

Courtney wrote about how her responding changed during the semester:

> I'm responding to what I read about the same amount but a lot deeper. My focus shifted from just taking the reading literally to thinking and analyzing it or making new comparisons to the world. Before, all my comparisons were to myself or other books and now they relate to the outside world. A lot of my previous journal entries were questions and I didn't respond to what I thought the answers were (which I do now). My recent journal entries have a lot more content than my older ones.

Ellen had an especially distinctive perspective:

> I like responding about books in my reading journal. I feel like I'm getting a chance to share my excitement with someone.

Dawn wrote about an aspect of response that never occurred to me:

> I think writing journal responses are making me a better reader because it makes me want to find out something interesting about my book to write about and trying to find something interesting makes me read more carefully.

Maci showed specifically how responding has helped her:

> I usually understand what I am reading, and, if I don't, I'll write it in my response. The response helps me just stop and think about what I just read.

And Nick's response illustrates how reading journals make students accountable:

> I am reading way more than I did last year. The reason why is, in 7th grade I was just told I had to read and do nothing else. However, this year I have to write about what I read and comprehend; this way I can't just say that I read. . . . The best part is, due to all the reading I've been doing, I have become more fluent and understand what I read better.

The majority of students perceived that reading response had contributed to making them more fluent, more thoughtful readers. I must admit that I was surprised that, given a chance to express displeasure with nightly writing, only two students took the no-risk opportunity to complain and convey that they felt response had not facilitated better reading.

## End-of-Year Reflection

At the end of the year, the students are given a last opportunity to leaf through the Reading Journals that they have maintained for a year. I request that they look at their Books Read Record(s), Daily Logs, and Journal entries and consider four questions:

1. How much did I read this year?

2. Did I meet or surpass my reading goals: Number of books and variety of genres?

3. When do I read the most? The least?

4. How has the response journal helped my reading, or how have my responses changed over the year?

Here are some samples of the students' reflections:

> My journal entries from the beginning of the year are much shorter from now. My journal entries now are about twice as long. In the beginning of the year in my journal entries I told about the book. Now I talk about how I feel about what is happening in the story and to the characters. In the beginning of the year I responded in my journal after I read, now I do it as I read and when I have a question or comment about a part as soon as I read it. This year I enjoyed having to read and respond every night, because I would never do that on my own and it made me realize how much I really enjoy reading. I also enjoyed the book

clubs & shared novel because I got to talk to other people about how they feel about the book.

—Chrissy

I am a more alert reader than in the beginning of the year. I actually look for figurative language now.

—Terrell

I can see that when I liked a book I read more and much faster, but when I didn't like a book I read it much slower. . . . I enjoyed reading journals because it let me reflect and think of what I just read and what is going on in the book.

—Kelsey

I think I have become a better reader because now I don't only just read, but I think it through, what the text means.

—Jen

This year I realized I looked more in depth to what I was reading. I tried to predict more and put myself in the characters' shoes. I tried to read different types of books but the main genre I read was realistic fiction. . . . In the reading journals, I realized that I was trying to relate the book to my life more compared to other years. I realized I wrote more if I was really interested in the book. . . . I realized that at the beginning of the year, my journals were pretty much summaries and as the year went on I got more in depth with what was happening in the book. I also realize that teen realistic fiction books are the books that I understand and comprehend the most.

—Cheryl

As a whole, I feel as though I have matured as a reader and as a writer, and I have noticed that as I am reading nowadays, I am predicting and thinking and trying to further understand what I am reading. I enjoyed the whole reading journal experience, and If I had time, I would definitely do it again.

—Kyle

However, I believe that as the year went by, the depth and thought [of my entries] was deeper. I was not just stating the obvious. I think I did improve about thinking deeply about what I read.

—Barbara

I have to say I've evolved as a reader. I think it's because reflecting on reading really got me thinking about what I read. Now it was more than just words in a book. It was like entering a different world every time I picked up a book.

—Carly

I liked the different styles of things than just writing a summary each time. Sometimes I would say my feelings towards things or a poem or another style of writing. There was a lot of freedom with the Reading Journals.

—Sean

My reading and responding has changed because I'm reading faster and more every night. I've read a lot of cool genres. In the beginning of the year my response was summarys and now with the Post-its it makes it easier for me. I liked the book clubs because reading with a group was fun. My favorite skill is the Post-it notes because instead of stopping to write on the response paper you can just write it on the Post-it note. The double-entry journal was the most effective on my reading because it helped me write more and really think about why the author put that in their book.

—Tyler

My reading from the beginning of the year until now has been improving. Not only has my reading become more fluent but I am responding better now. The length of the responses are staying the same but the responses are more in depth. Before I used to summarize the chapter a lot, but now I am focusing on more than just a summary. I am reflecting on the characters a lot and how the author constructs his/her writing. I have read a lot of books this year and I am not fixed on one genre like before. Also I feel that I think more when I read about what I am reading.

—Amanda

No student confirmed the value of reader response more eloquently than John:

Reading journals have really helped me think deeper into the story. Stopping every 25 minutes to write allows me to reflect on the character's actions, make connections, and understand why the author writes the way he does. I have also been exploring different genres of literature during my reading journals this year. I have read sports, adventure, mystery, historical fiction, short story collections, and comedy. Not only has reading journals helped me in just my reading comprehension, but it also has improved my writing skills. Analyzing the author's style influences my own methods of writing.

I could not have said it better myself. However, what is important was that, upon self-reflection, it was a student who said it. Not only do these sentiments show metacognition but the values of reading journals and reader response.

# 12

# Coming to a Conclusion

It wasn't until I was building a house that I noticed roofs. Sure, on a subconscious level, I knew that all houses had roofs, but I'd never *noticed* them. When we had to make a decision about our roof, suddenly every roof I passed became worthy of note. I noticed color. *Red roofs definitely don't go with yellow houses. Green with yellow? Not bad.* I analyzed materials. *What about a copper roof? How long before it turns green?? What are the advantages? Besides price, what are the disadvantages? How does rain sound on a metal roof? Will it keep me up all night?* I looked at shapes and visualized roofs with my building plans. *Gables? Peaks? Flat top? Slope? Will we have leaves that have to be swept off?*

I employed the same strategies as readers. I had an authentic purpose for observing, and I activated existing knowledge from houses in which I had lived. I had questions and made connections. I drew inferences and made predictions about materials, shapes, and costs. I judged the reliability of contractors' suggestions. I learned building jargon. I made notes about what I noticed on my walks through my neighborhood and my rides through other neighborhoods. I reflected, and I responded. Then I moved on to doors.

This is what a reading response program does for readers. We notice whatever becomes significant in our lives. That is why it is imperative that teachers make response significant in their students' lives. My students could read, some better than others. Response does not teach students to read; response trains them to read better. Response trains students to notice.

I find that I use the terms *notice* and *note* more and more frequently as the year progresses.

"*Notice* anything in your novels that connects to an experience that you have had and *note* it in your journal."

"*Notice* what text features are in the article you are reading and *note* how they help you comprehend the article better."

"*Notice* how the authors describe the characters, *note* what techniques they use, and then try to imitate those techniques in your own narrative writing."

As readers notice and note, they are thinking about the text, their reading strategies, literary elements, and, eventually, author's craft. They find they are comprehending better and more, and their reading becomes richer and their thinking more profound. Most students perceive that they are enjoying reading more than ever, and they seem puzzled by this. Quite a few of my students commented that they were upset that I expected them to read over the winter break but then found they read even more than I had required. One student said that reading became contagious and that her family read with her.

One might assume that, with all this responding, students would read less. They actually read more. At midyear, many students have surpassed their goals for the year—both in the amount of books read and the variety of genres read, and the majority have read more than half their goal. They based their goals on readings from previous years.

Readers notice to become better readers. They note so that I can assess their reading—both to formulate future lessons and to evaluate their comprehension. And they note so that they can reflect back on their reading and responses.

When students reflect on their reading, they gain ownership of their "write" to read.

# Resource A

## LITERACY REFERENCES

### Chapter 2

Mitch Albom, *The Five People You Meet in Heaven*

Stacy Cretzmeyer, *Your Name Is Renee*

Walter Dean Myers, *Monster*

David Peltzer, *A Child Called "It": One Child's Courage to Survive*

Sonya Sones, *Stop Pretending*

Jeannette Walls, *The Glass Castle*

### Chapter 3

Mark Dunn, *Ella Minnow Pea*

Donald Sobol, *Encyclopedia Brown Shows the Way*

Gabrielle Zevin, *Elsewhere*

### Chapter 4

Phyllis Reynolds Naylor, *Dangerously Alice*

Ernest Lawrence Thayer, "Casey at the Bat"

### Chapter 5

Paul Fleischman (with Eric Beddows, illustrator), *Joyful Noise: Poems for Two Voices*

Sheila Gordon, *Waiting for the Rain*

Dara Horn, "Walking with Living Feet," in *Merlyn's Pen* (October/November 1993), pp. 1–3

Lois Lowry, *The Giver*

Salman Rushdie, *Haroun and the Sea of Stories*

Esmeralda Santiago, *When I Was Puerto Rican*

## Chapter 6

Bette Greene, *Summer of My German Soldier*

Margaret Peterson Haddix, *Among the Betrayed*

Betty Merti, "Nazi Terror Moves to Holland," in *The World of Anne Frank: A Complete Resource Guide*

Gail Newman, "An Anti-Semitic Demonstration"

## Chapter 7

Frank Bonham, *Durango Street*

Lois Duncan, *Down a Dark Hall*

Walter Dean Myers, *Hoops*

## Chapter 8

Mitch Albom, *For One More Day*

Laurie Halse Anderson, *Twisted*

Joan Bauer, *Hope Was Here*

Dan Brown, *The DaVinci Code*

S. E. Hinton, *Tex*

Anthony Horowitz, *Stormbreaker*

Antony Johnston, *Stormbreaker* (graphic novel adaptation)

Gregory Maguire, *Mirror, Mirror*

Donna Jo Napoli, *Stones in the Water*

William Shakespeare, *Othello*

Paul Zindel, *The Pigman*

## Chapter 9

Jenna Bush, *Ana's Story*

Charles Dickens, *Oliver Twist*

Jeanne DuPrau, *The Diamond of Darkhold*

Paula Fox, *Monkey Island*

Norma Fox Mazer, *After the Rain*

Stephenie Meyer, *Twilight*

Gloria D. Miklowitz, *The War Between the Classes*

Katherine Paterson, *Lyddie*

Elizabeth George Speare, *The Witch of Blackbird Pond*

Daniel Waters, *Generation Dead*

## Chapter 10

Diane Hart, "Chapter 30: The Cold War," in *History Alive! The United States*

Henry Wadsworth Longfellow, "The Midnight Ride of Paul Revere"

Lois Ruby, *Steal Away Home*

Amelie Welden, *Girls Who Rocked the World*

## Chapter 11

Mitch Albom, *The Five People You Meet in Heaven*

Stephenie Meyer, *Twilight*

Donna Jo Napoli, *Daughter of Venice*

Donna Jo Napoli, *Stones in the Water*

# Resource B

## FORMS AND EXAMPLES

# I. Independent Reading Requirements

## Assignment Expectation and Rationale

To create a literate environment in our language arts classroom and to make each student a better reader and writer, each student will be expected to read and respond in writing *25 minutes each day, 5 days per week.* You are to read books—fiction or nonfiction—of your choice and write short personal reactions in a journal. You will be graded on the amount of time you read and the quality of your response. Response writing will be taught in class.

## Choosing Books

Although you may read any books that are on your reading level, you will be encouraged to read a variety of genres and authors. Choose books on topics or in genres that interest you but also branch out. You do not have to finish a book that you are not enjoying. If you find that you do not like a book, you may abandon it; you should know after a few chapters if you are enjoying a book.

There are many paperback novels in our classroom. Borrowing those books or books from the library should make purchasing books unnecessary. If you have any paperbacks you no longer want or need, we are always looking for contributions for our classroom library.

At times we will have book passes so that you can become familiar with the classroom library, and book talks will familiarize you with books that your classmates are reading. The class library also contains a binder of Reading Recommendations that you are invited to look through or contribute to.

## Response Journals

You will need a two-pocket, three-prong folder with a few sheets of composition paper. This will be your Reading Journal. You will be given a Daily Log sheet and a Record of Book Read and Genre Chart to put in your Journal and keep up-to-date. Other reading forms will be added during the year.

Your response to your reading is a personal reaction to *anything* you read or think about when reading. This is not to be a summary of the story. You may react in your reading journal in any format you wish—prose, poetry, letters to me or to the author, or, if appropriate, drawings, etc. You will be given credit for each reading and entry. Each entry should be a five-minute response, which will be about one-third page; some days you will have more to write, some days less. I will try to read all responses but at minimum will read and respond to one journal entry chosen by you (with an *) each week. Sometimes you will be asked to choose an entry for a classmate or a parent to respond to.

Each day you will log in the date, title, amount of time spent reading, and the page numbers read. Each Journal entry should contain the date and your written response.

## When to Read

You are to read as homework for 25 minutes. You should always have your book with you in case there is time to read in my class or other classes, but if you do not have your book, you may read and respond to newspaper or magazine articles (once or twice a week).

Hopefully, we will have some time to read in class many days. This is considered *extra* reading time and does not require separate written responses. When the class is reading a shared novel or when you are involved in book club reading, that reading will constitute your reading and response assignments.

## Grading

You will receive points weekly for amount of reading accomplished and the amount of reading response (5 nights' reading + 5 responses = 100%) as a quiz grade. You may also receive grades, from time to time, based on brief, informal book talks done in class or assignments based on your book. If you do not keep up with your reading, you will not be able to participate in some of these activities and assignments. The Reading and Response Journal will be a large part of your grade, as it is a very important component of our curriculum.

Please take thoughtful advantage of the chance to choose your own reading.

## 2. Daily Reading Log

| Date | Title | Genre | Pages Read | Time Read | Focus Lesson |
|------|-------|-------|------------|-----------|--------------|
|      |       |       | to         |           |              |
|      |       |       |            |           |              |
|      |       |       |            |           |              |
|      |       |       |            |           |              |
|      |       |       |            |           |              |
|      |       |       |            |           |              |
|      |       |       |            |           |              |
|      |       |       |            |           |              |
|      |       |       |            |           |              |
|      |       |       |            |           |              |
|      |       |       |            |           |              |
|      |       |       |            |           |              |
|      |       |       |            |           |              |
|      |       |       |            |           |              |
|      |       |       |            |           |              |
|      |       |       |            |           |              |
|      |       |       |            |           |              |
|      |       |       |            |           |              |
|      |       |       |            |           |              |
|      |       |       |            |           |              |
|      |       |       |            |           |              |

## 3. Response Starters

I noticed . . .

I was really surprised . . .

I wonder why . . .

I didn't understand . . .

I began to think . . .

Something new I learned . . .

I am guessing that . . .

I felt _____ when . . .

I couldn't believe . . .

My favorite part was . . .

If I were [character] . . .

What I found interesting . . .

What I think will happen is . . .

I like the way . . .

A question I have . . .

I think the author . . .

This reminds me of . . .

I can picture . . .

I predict . . .

The author is saying . . .

I never thought . . .

I began to think of . . .

I know the feeling . . .

My favorite _____ is . . .

I don't/didn't like . . .

I can imagine . . .

What I thought would happen was . . .

I think _____ will become important.

## 4. Reading Interests (for Recommendations)

| TOPICS | GENRES | AUTHORS |
|---|---|---|
| Example: Baseball | Example: Fantasy | Example: Natasha Friend |
|  |  |  |

## Book Pass: Books for Future Reading

| TITLE | AUTHOR | GENRE |
|---|---|---|
|  |  |  |
|  |  |  |
|  |  |  |
|  |  |  |
|  |  |  |
|  |  |  |
|  |  |  |
|  |  |  |
|  |  |  |
|  |  |  |

## 5. Double-Entry Journal—Questioning

Date _____     Title _____     Pages _____ to _____

Summary: _____

_____

_____

| From the **BOOK**<br>Character, Setting, Event, Quote | From Your **BRAIN**<br>Your Questions | Page |
|---|---|---|
| 1. | | _____ |
| | | |
| | | |
| | | |
| | | |
| 2. | | _____ |
| | | |
| | | |
| | | |
| | | |
| 3. | | _____ |
| | | |
| | | |
| | | |
| | | |

## 6. Question-Answer Chart

| Question | Answer | Where Found | Strategy Used: Another Text; Rereading; Reference Materials; Inference |
|---|---|---|---|
|  |  |  |  |
|  |  |  |  |
|  |  |  |  |
|  |  |  |  |
|  |  |  |  |
|  |  |  |  |
|  |  |  |  |
|  |  |  |  |
|  |  |  |  |
|  |  |  |  |
|  |  |  |  |
|  |  |  |  |
|  |  |  |  |
|  |  |  |  |
|  |  |  |  |

## 7. Strategies Used by Successful Readers

1. Determine a **purpose** for reading.

2. Activate **existing knowledge.**

3. Ask **questions** of the text before, during, and after reading.

4. Make **connections** from the text to readers' lives, to other texts, and to the world.

5. Draw **inferences** from the text.

6. **Visualize** or create other sensory images.

7. Determine which details are **important** and judge the **narrator's reliability.**

8. Make **predictions** based on inferences.

9. **Monitor** comprehension (**summarize**).

10. Use **fix-up** strategies:

    - **Rereading**

    - **Vocabulary**

    - **Text features**

    - **Adjusting reading rate**

## 8. Double-Entry Journal—Making Connections

Date _____     Title _____     Pages _____ to _____

Summary: _____

_____

_____

| From the **BOOK**<br>Character, Setting, Event, Quote | From Your **BRAIN**<br>Connection | Type<br>Self, Text, World |
|---|---|---|
| 1. | | _____ |
| | | |
| | | |
| | | |
| | | |
| 2. | | _____ |
| | | |
| | | |
| | | |
| | | |
| 3. | | _____ |
| | | |
| | | |
| | | |
| | | |

## 9. Double-Entry Journal—Literary Elements

Name _____  Date _____  Text _____

Summary:————————————————————————————————————————

_____

_____

| From the **BOOK** | From Your **BRAIN**<br>Your personal response, inference, questions |
|---|---|
| 1. Protagonist's Character Traits | |
| | |
| | |
| | |
| 2. Setting: Time/Place/Atmosphere | |
| | |
| | |
| | |
| 3. Conflict | |
| | |
| | |
| | |
| 4. Writing Style/POV | |
| | |
| | |
| | |

## 10. Double-Entry Journal—Identifying Strategies Used

Date _____     Title _____     Chapter_____

Summary: _____

_____

_____

| From the **BOOK**<br>Character, Setting, Event, Quote | From your **BRAIN**<br>Your Personal Response | Strategy |
|---|---|---|
| 1. | | _____ |
| | | |
| | | |
| | | |
| | | |
| 2. | | _____ |
| | | |
| | | |
| | | |
| | | |
| 3. | | _____ |
| | | |
| | | |
| | | |

## 11. Sticky-Note Response Journal

Date _____ Title _____ Pages _____ to _____

## 12. Sticky-Note Question-Answer-Response Journal

| Questions I Had While Reading | Answers Found | Comment |
|---|---|---|
| | | |

## 13. Book Club Meeting Agenda

1. You must have your book and your completed double-entry journal.

2. After the opening whole-class focus lesson and any announcements, club members arrange their desks into circles.

3. Distribute homework response sheets from last lesson and add to your individual Reading Journals.

4. Designate a Collector to collect current homework and to distribute Reflection sheets at the end of the meeting.

5. Book club meeting (20–25 minutes):

   Using your notes and books, discuss the chapters read.

   Follow our class guidelines for supportive, productive discussions and listening.

   If appropriate, integrate the *focus lesson* into your discussion.

   Add meeting notes to the front of your current journal form.

   When finished, make any adjustments to the club reading schedule.

   Collect double-entry journal forms, deposit them in the homework bin, and distribute Reflection forms.

6. *5 minutes:* Move desks back to position and *individually* fill out Book Club Reflection sheets as specifically as possible; comments will be kept confidential.

7. If any class time remains, continue reading your novel until the end of the period. Incorporate the day's *focus lesson* into your reading response.

Hand in your personal reflections on the way out.

## 14. Book Club Double-Entry Response Journal

Name _____   Novel _____

For Meeting Date _____   Chapters _____   Pages _____ to _____

Summary: _____

_____

_____

_____

_____

_____

_____

_____

_____

_____

_____

_____

Focus Lesson: _____

Notes: _____

_____

_____

_____

_____

_____

_____

_____

_____

_____

| From the **BOOK**<br>Character, Setting, Event, Quote | From Your **BRAIN**<br>Your Personal **Response** |
|---|---|
| 1. Discussion question or point: | |
| | |
| | |
| | |
| 2. Interesting quote, snapshot, figurative language, character: | |
| | |
| | |
| | |
| 3. Vocabulary word, definition, and sentence it appeared in: | |
| | |
| | |
| | |
| 4. Question, prediction, inference: | |
| | |
| | |
| | |

## 15. Responses to Author's Craft

This week, copy from your reading examples of *Good writing*:

- Detailed, sensory descriptions of characters or settings
- Authentic-sounding dialogue; use of dialect, jargon, or regional accent
- Interesting use of punctuation or words
- Strong verbs, specific nouns, and the sentences in which they appear
- Figurative language

Independent Reading Journal Entry # _____     Date _____     Page _____

_____

_____

_____

_____

_____

_____

_____

_____

Your comment/response to this writing:

_____

_____

_____

_____

_____

_____

_____

_____

_____

_____

## 16. Reading Strategies—Author's Craft Response Journal

Date: _____     Pages _____ to _____

Title: _____     Author: _____

**What I Read** (brief summary):

_____

_____

_____

_____

_____

_____

**How I Read** (What reading strategies you used—Give specific examples from your book.):

_____

_____

_____

_____

_____

_____

**How It Was Written** (What you noticed about writer's craft—Give specific examples from your book.):

_____

_____

_____

_____

_____

## 17. News Article Formats

I keep six honest serving men

(They taught me all I knew);

Their names are WHAT and WHY and WHEN

And HOW and WHERE and WHO.

> —Rudyard Kipling

### News

HEADLINE

Byline

Dateline

¶1: Who, What, Where, When, Why/How

¶2: Additional Details

¶3: More Information

¶4: Interview or Quote

Picture

### Human Interest

HEADLINE

¶1: Interest-Grabbing Opening

Who, What, Where, When, Why/How

¶2: Additional Details About the 5 Ws

¶3: More Information

¶4: Interview or Quote

### People Poll

QUESTION that includes Who, What, Where, When, Why/How

Background Information

Picture of Interviewees

Names, Ages

Occupations

City, State of Residences

Answers and Reasons

### Advice Column

DEAR _____:

¶1: Who, What, Where, When, Why/How

¶2: Background or History of Situation

¶3: Solutions Tried or Considered

Advice Sought

Pseudonym

¶4: Answer—Advice

### Editorial or Commentary

¶1: ISSUE:

Who, What, Where, When, Why/How

[Follows format for a persuasive essay.]

### Obituary

HEADLINE: Name, age, profession

¶1: Name, Age, Residence, Profession, "died"

When, Where

¶2: Short Biographical Sketch:

"born . . . ," "lived . . . ," "worked . . ."

¶3: Memberships, Community Involvement,

Hobbies, Volunteer Activities

¶4: Family Relationships, "survived by . . ."

¶5: Funeral, Viewing/Mass, Burial:

places—dates—times

¶6: Flowers/Contributions "in lieu of flowers"

## Police Report

HEADLINE

¶1: Who, What, When, Where, Why/How

¶2: Information about "Arrest" and "Charges"

¶3: Details of Accusation/Crime

¶4: Details of Hearing or Trial

¶5: Interview with Victim, Defendant, Police, Witnesses, or Neighbors

## Classified Ads

FOR SALE—Articles or Real Estate

Item(s)

Description, Condition

Price

Reason for Selling

Phone Number, Name of Seller or Agent

POSITION WANTED

Job

Hours Available

Education/Certifications

Past Experience

Salary Required

Name, Phone, or P.O. Box

## Political Cartoon

Who, What, Where, When, Why, or How in picture or in caption

Cartoon must "state" opinion on a situation.

## 18. Content Area Double-Entry Response Journal

Subject _____  Chapter _____  Pages _____ to _____

| From the **TEXT** (facts, quotes) | From Your **BRAIN** (thoughts, reactions, opinions) | Page |
|---|---|---|
| 1. | | |
| | | |
| | | |
| | | |
| | | |
| 2. | | |
| | | |
| | | |
| | | |
| 3. | | |
| | | |
| | | |
| | | |
| 4. | | |
| | | |
| | | |
| | | |

# References

Bauer, J. (2002). *Hope was here.* New York: Puffin Books, Penguin Putnam. (Original work published 2000)

Beers, K. (2003). *When kids can't read—What teachers can do: A guide for teachers 6–12.* Portsmouth, NH: Heinemann.

Bloom, B. S. (1956). *Taxonomy of educational objectives, handbook 1: Cognitive domain.* New York: Addison-Wesley.

Booth, D. (2001). *Reading & writing in the middle years.* Portland, ME: Stenhouse.

Calkins, L. M. (2001). *The art of teaching reading.* New York: Longman, Addison-Wesley Educational.

Daniels, H. (2002). *Literature circles: Voice and choice in the student-centered classroom.* Portland, ME: Stenhouse.

Fountas, I. C., & Pinnell, G. S. (2000). *Guiding readers and writers (Grades 3–6): Teaching comprehension, genre, and content literacy.* Portsmouth, NH: Heinemann.

Harvey, S., & Goudvis, A. (2000). *Strategies that work: Teaching comprehension to enhance understanding.* Portland, ME: Stenhouse.

National Reading Panel. (2000). *Teaching children to read; An evidence-based assessment of the scientific research literature on reading and its implications for reading instruction; Reports of the subgroups* (NIH Publication No. 00-4754). Rockville, MD: National Institute of Child Health and Human Development. Available March 31, 2009, at http://www.nationalreadingpanel.org/Publications/publications.htm

Netting, J. F. (2005, February 1). The kind of face only a wasp could trust. *Discover Magazine,* 10.

Probst, R. (1994). Reader response theory and the English curriculum. *English Journal, 83*(3), 37–44.

Rosenblatt, L. M. (1978). *The reader, the text, the poem: The transactional theory of the literary work.* Carbondale: Southern Illinois University Press.

Rosenblatt, L. M. (2005a). From *Literature as exploration. Voices from the Middle, 12*(3), p. 27. (Reprinted from *Literature as exploration,* 1938, New York: MLA)

Rosenblatt, L. M. (2005b). Retrospect. *Voices from the Middle, 12*(3), pp. 13–19.

Routman, R. (2000). *Conversations: Strategies for teaching, learning, and evaluating.* Portsmouth, NH: Heinemann.

Scottoline, L. (2002). *Mistaken identity.* New York: Harpertorch. (Original work published 1999)

Sonnenblick, J. (2007). *Notes from the midnight driver.* New York: Scholastic. (Original work published 2006)

Wilhelm, J. (1997). *You gotta be the book.* New York: Teachers College Press.

Wormeli, R. (2006). Accountability: Teaching through assessment and feedback, not grading. *American Secondary Education, 34*(3), 14–27.

Zinsser, W. (1988). *Writing to learn.* New York: Harper & Row.

# Credits

All photos are used with permission of photographer J. Douglas Tyson.

Chapter 4: Vinz, Mark. "What I Remember About the 6th Grade." From *Late Night Calls* by Mark Vinz (New Rivers Press). Copyright 1992 by Mark Vinz and reprinted by permission of the author.

Chapter 5: Poems by Mary Scaperotto and Amanda Wochele, along with quotes from the "Poems in Two Voices" section of Chapter 5, appeared in Lesley Roessing's (2005) "Creating Empathetic Connections to Literature" from *The Quarterly of the National Writing Project* 27(2), 7–11. These are reprinted with permission from the National Writing Project (NWP). The mission of NWP is to improve the teaching of writing and improve learning in the nation's schools. Explore NWP's resources at www.nwp.org.

Chapter 5: Text of the identification cards included courtesy of United States Holocaust Memorial Museum.

Chapter 9: Hutt, Rachel. "Book Review of *Twilight*." An edited version of this review appeared in *Voices from the Middle, 15*(4), March 2008. Copyright 2008 by the National Council of Teachers of English. Reprinted with permission.

# Index

# CORWIN

A SAGE Company